PRAISE FOR *THE SACRED PULSE: HOLY RHYTHMS FOR OVERWHELMED SOULS*

"Filled with honest and often winsome accounts of her own struggles to attune her daily life to the movement of God in the world, the book draws on a wealth of spiritual insight to help readers retreat from the busyness of life and recenter their lives around rhythms that heal, restore, and sustain. The result is as refreshing as it is compelling."

—Kristin Kobes Du Mez, *New York Times*
bestselling author of *Jesus and John Wayne*

"I felt seen by this book, in a way that was uncomfortable at first. The unsettling insight into my frenetic performance for God was the opening I needed to hear April Fiet's invitation: to learn to dance with God again, finding rhythms that are, paradoxically, like rest in motion."

—James K. A. Smith, author of *You Are What You Love* and *On the Road with Saint Augustine*

"*The Sacred Pulse* encourages readers to move away from a life of mere to-do list actions and into living the pure aspiration of who we are and what we really want our lives to be. She shows how to find our way to wholeness through intention, community, creativity, and a life-giving embrace of sacred time. The rhythm of this book can be heard as a joyous dance to which we are all invited."

—Sophfronia Scott, author of *The Seeker and the Monk: Everyday Conversations with Thomas Merton*

"April Fiet is the type of pastor and writer who inspires me to be fully human and to experience the miracle of God's grace in gardening, good friends, and welcome gentleness in our complex lives."

—Jes Kast, pastor of Faith United Church of Christ

"Learning a sacred rhythm for your unique life and needs is a cruical spritiual practice—a lifelong habit that nurtures spiritual formation and wholeness. April Fiet's book offers us life."

> —Lisa Colón DeLay, author of *The Wild Land Within* and the host of the *Spark My Muse* podcast

"April Fiet gives practical, profound, and transformational observations, calling us to join the sacred dance and to listen to the daily holy rhythm of God's heart. If you are weary and worn out, or simply in need of refreshing, read *The Sacred Pulse* and renew your soul."

> —Douglas S. Bursch, co-pastor of Evergreen Church and author of *Posting Peace*

"We have plenty of books on methods, but April Fiet shows how to grow in your awareness of the sacred in the simple, unexpected areas of your life."

> —Ed Cyzewski, author of *Reconnect* and *Flee, Be Silent, Pray*

"Filled with clever observations and thoughtful ideas both large and small, this book is a wonderful companion for those of us who want to reorient ourselves to healthy Kingdom rhythms but are unsure of where to start."

> —Chandra Crane, author of *Mixed Blessing* and national mixed ministry coordinator for InterVarsity Christian Fellowship

"In *The Sacred Pulse*, April Fiet gently invites us to witness how she has exited echo chambers, hit pause on mindless consumption, and questioned her loyalty to the notion of independence, replacing these with simple, life-giving observations and practices that bring wholeness and spark justice. Her reflections on snow days, backyard chickens, and so much more filled me with gratitude for the divine rhythm that gives us life."

> —Jennifer Grant, author of *Dimming the Day*

THE
SACRED
PULSE

THE
SACRED
PULSE

**HOLY RHYTHMS FOR
OVERWHELMED SOULS**

APRIL FIET

Broadleaf Books
Minneapolis

THE SACRED PULSE
Holy Rhythms for Overwhelmed Souls

Cover image: iStock
Cover design: Lindsey Owens

Print ISBN: 978-1-5064-6908-9
eBook ISBN: 978-1-5064-6909-6

To Jeff, Jakob, and Malia,
What a delight to dance through life with you.

CONTENTS

PART III
THE DANCE OF BELONGING

PART IV
THE DANCE OF RENEWAL

FOREWORD

Our hearts long for an elusive wholeness. Sometimes this wholeness feels like a distant memory—a faint whisper amid a cacophony of beeps and buzzes from our devices and the meaningless chatter of pundits. In the busiest moments of our lives, we may lose touch with it altogether, tossed in the waves of urgency and obligation. And yet the beckoning never ceases: to oneness, to worthiness, to an intimacy we dare only dream of.

Our longing awakens during a long drive through the country, alert to the expanse of rolling hills that draw us out of our anxious limbic brain into prefrontal presence. Our hearts rouse when we look into the face of a newborn baby, or when a chevron of migrating Canada geese fly overhead, or when a song elicits tears. Soon enough we're lost again in a flurry of urgent texts or breaking news of more racial injustice. Our nervous systems rev up into sympathetic activation, cortisol and adrenaline readying the body for battle.

But we long to long again. And if we can slow our beating hearts and attend to the hidden wholeness around us, we find ourselves attuning again to the rhythms of creation.

If you long to long again, April Fiet is a guide I'd commend to you. April knows the fury of life's demands—she's a pastor and a mother, after all. Her days are marked by anxious asks and insistent emails and tedious texts. What is remarkable about her story is that she hasn't lost the plotline. Her invitation to participate in rhythms of renewal is also a refusal to succumb to a story that ends in the thorns and fig leaves of Genesis 3, where shame and self-protection breed hopelessness. Mind you, she knows this territory. She knows what it feels like to not be enough, do enough, perform well enough. She hears the same voices in her head that you and I do! But she's listened more closely to that whisper of original goodness and wholeness—in the garden, the kitchen, and even in the grocery store. Amid shifting seasons, she can offer a word of attunement, invitation, and hope.

I believe her words are desperately needed today. We're as anxious and as disconnected as we've ever been. We doomscroll through Instagram and Facebook and Twitter even in the first moments of morning alertness, as April notes, awakened by the blue light of a device rather than the rising sun. We're desperate for new rhythms, and they're literally available to us in our everyday life if we'll only pay attention: in a vulnerable connection with a beloved friend, in patient attentiveness to your garden, in the liturgy of the church year, in a renewed sense of *kairos* time in a *chronos* world, and in the deep rest your soul needs. April is your spiritual director for this journey, a wise guide into the open country of a wholehearted life. She invites you to pay attention, to rediscover your heart's longing. Wholeness isn't as elusive as you might think.

The Sacred Pulse is not meant to be devoured in one sitting. I invite you to marinate in it, and to approach each chapter as a living invitation to a slower, deeper life in God's remarkably generative and good creation. While the content is rich, April's invitation to an embodied wholeness in your everyday life is even more satisfying. May her wisdom and good guidance be a different kind of alert: not in the form of a beep or a buzz, but the word of a kind friend inviting you to taste and see the goodness of God.

—Chuck DeGroat, therapist, professor at Western
Theological Seminary, and author of
Wholeheartedness: Busyness, Exhaustion,
and Healing the Divided Self

INTRODUCTION

B efore you can learn to play a musical instrument, you first have to learn about the beat. When I was five or six years old, I would climb up onto the piano bench at my grandparents' house. My feet would dangle above the short, cream-colored carpet as I sat, and I would reach for their old-fashioned metronome. The almost pyramid-shaped apparatus felt grown-up and mysterious. After fumbling with my fingers, I would remove the metronome's cover. Carefully, I would slip the weight along the pendulum in the center. The closer the weight was to the base of the metronome, the faster the metronome would tick. When I pushed the weight clear out to the top of the pendulum, the metronome would slow down, the weight seeming to sway to a song I had not yet learned to play. Before I could take liberties with the rhythm, to move the music with inflection and imagination, I would first need to learn to play the notes to the movement of the beat.

The world has a rhythm that pulses and moves. It ebbs and flows; it nudges us to keep moving. We were created to step in time with this rhythm. When God made the world with the rhythms of night and day, moon and sun, water and dry land, God placed us into the midst of a creation that was just learning how to dance. In the garden, God gave the first human beings a commission to care for and tend to the rhythmic and beautiful world that was bursting with life. Boundaries were set when God commanded people not to eat from the tree of the knowledge of good and evil: not as a way to trap the people, but so they might discover the sacred pulse of God's world. God invited the people to move with the rhythm that would give them life, to trust in the divine way as the path to wholeness and peace. Instead, as Lisa Sharon Harper puts it, "humanity chose its own way." Rather than a loving dominion of the earth, the first humans chose domination and "self-interest above the interest of the other"—the aftermath of which was "sin, separation, and death." From the very beginning, the world was created with a rhythm of wholeness and vibrancy, but humanity chose a different way.

I have spent much of my life feeling like I was out of rhythm. In elementary school, the music teacher evaluated each of us to see where we might best fit in the music program. She explored rhythms and melodies with each of us individually, and then she made recommendations for students to be placed in either band or choir. When a student seemed to connect with a particular instrument or instrument family, she made a note of that too. On my evaluation, the teacher wrote something like, "April shows musical promise. She has a natural understanding of melodies and musical lines, but she has no rhythm whatsoever. She would do well in band but should not be assigned a percussion instrument." I went on to play clarinet in fifth-grade band, and I played clarinet in college as an aspiring clarinet performance major (until jaw problems sidelined that dream). Although it was far from instinctual, I eventually learned to play in step with the beat of the band.

While I celebrated finding the beat in music, I continued to struggle with discovering a rhythm in my own life. For a long time, I scapegoated the busy pace of society instead of getting to the root of my feelings of disconnection. I pictured the world around me as a chaotic place that was out of rhythm. In my imagination, I saw the world as skipping a beat, or awkwardly clapping on one and three instead of on two and four. I felt myself carried along by an unhealthy, unrelenting movement, and I idolized people who seemed to march to the beat of a different drummer. The people who were able to pry themselves away from the relentless, driving forces of everyday life inspired me to try to do the same for myself. Yet no matter how hard I tried to find the beat, I still found myself tripping over my own two feet. Somewhere inside of myself, I knew the rhythm I was marching to was not the only one or even the best one. But that offbeat, clapping-on-one-and-three kind of lifestyle is terribly hard to get out of once you are in it. The rhythm of wholeness and shalom and well-being eluded me. Try as I might, I found myself fumbling and faltering along with something else instead, something that didn't bring joy and flourishing.

I thought my problem was that I was too busy. I thought everyone was too busy. The COVID-19 pandemic tested that theory, and I realized that I had oversimplified the situation. As all of my evening meetings were canceled or moved online due to public health guidelines, and as all of my kids' extracurricular activities disappeared, I found that I still felt out of sorts. Perhaps the problem wasn't just the schedule I was keeping but something deeper still.

Since the dawn of time, human beings have found themselves moving in and out of step with the song of God. We experience moments, or even days at a time, when we are able to breathe deeply, step purposefully, and move intentionally in ways that bring us life and restoration. But if you are anything like me, those moments are short-lived. Even after we have experienced the movement and the sacred pulse of wholeness, we are urged to exchange it for the grind that leaves us depleted and wondering what it's all for. In the moments in which our footsteps connect with the song of the new creation, we know it in our bones. Then, just as quickly, we step away from justice and mercy, compassion and love, nourishment and wholeness, and choose what will never last or satisfy. What if we found the courage to listen again for the rhythm that will cause us to thrive? What if we stepped out of our ruts and habits on the off chance that what we will find is what we have always needed?

When we think about the rhythm of the world, we might think about the frenetic pace of looming deadlines or the stress of having more to do than can possibly fit into the hours we are given each day. We might think about promotions and career options, big decisions and impossible expectations. We might feel tempted to measure our lives against the lives of our neighbors or to compare ourselves to people in similar stages of life and feel the need to move a little faster and work a little (or a lot) harder to keep up. I have used words like *breakneck, overwhelming,* and *too much* to describe my life.

After seminary, when I transitioned into life as a pastor of a rural congregation, I thought the scattered, overwhelming pace of my life would slow down and fall into place. Thirteen years of pastoral ministry later and I realized the problem wasn't my circumstances; it was the rhythm I expected myself to follow. In those early years of ministry, I started my blog—*At the Table*—and began writing on Twitter to share my thoughts about the struggles of seeking to slow down in a too-fast world. I wrote about baking bread and taking walks, about crocheting and caring for my backyard chickens, and I found a community of people who were longing, just as I was, to hear the song of God sung over us again, to walk in step with a rhythm that brings wholeness and life.

For too many days, I looked at my life as a series of tasks to complete or boxes to check, and I felt defeated every night as I fell into bed with my to-do list unfinished. More times than I can count, I measured my worth by how many things I accomplished or how I thought I looked in the eyes of others. I moved and struggled and wrestled along with the rhythm of what I thought others expected, the pace that I thought everyone else was keeping too. And I found myself exhausted. I began to realize that the rhythm we are called to follow has less to do with what we *do* and much more to do with who we *are*.

Unfortunately, it often takes coming to the end of our own abilities before we stop to listen for a better way. We tend to wait until we are desperate and run ragged before we muster up the courage to step away from familiar but destructive habits. The tragedy of the breakneck pace of an out-of-rhythm life is that we spend much of our time missing out on the poetry and pulse of the created world. What if, instead of running on vapors, we allowed ourselves to listen for the rhythm of well-being—the one still resounding within our hearts even when we've become very skilled at not listening?

The sacred pulse of the world has nothing to do with endless to-do lists, arbitrary measures of success, or the pace to which we subject ourselves daily. We might have worked to tune our lives to the song we think others expect us to sing. We might have become experts at setting up obstacles and barriers to listening to creation's song. But despite our best efforts to the contrary, I believe God is still whispering to us over all the din that we are beloved. God is inviting us to let go of our impossible expectations for ourselves, to let go of the feelings of shame and worthlessness, and to find our way back to the song that will heal our deepest wounds and lead us to dance.

In Genesis, we encounter the story of creation as poetry. The creation poem utilizes repetition to give us a taste of the movement and pulse of God's good world. Phrases like "there was evening and there was morning," "and it was so," and "God said" invite us to experience the rhythm for ourselves. Genesis 1 was not written in poetic form to minimize the work of creation but instead to teach us that life was not created haphazardly. Creation was expansive and imaginative, breathtaking and inspiring. Creation was also orderly and rhythmic in the movement from day to night, the separation of the water from the land, and the repeated refrain that all of it was good.

The created world still moves with a pulse and a rhythm that is meant to be the heartbeat of all we do. The rhythm of creation is intended to be our rhythm, the movement and beat the undercurrent that guides our feet. This rhythm cannot be captured in five easy steps or distilled into three points, a poem, and a prayer. We will get it wrong a lot. But the invitation remains. Will we learn to dance, or will we stumble along to our own beat?

This book is the fruit of having lived an unbalanced life for way too long. I have felt exhausted despite getting more than enough sleep every night—not physically tired, but weary inside. I have struggled to fit everything into each day, and I have fallen into bed night after night so tired that I fall asleep as soon as my head hits the pillow. I always thought that I was one of those people who needed things to be just so in my life in order to function at my best. I imagined that some people were just better able to work long days, get little sleep, and eat junk food all day long with little in the way of consequences. I have begun to realize that this isn't true. Some of us are better at hiding our weariness than others, but all of us thrive when we step away from the rhythm of expectations and tasks and toward the rhythm that gives us life. When we are moving in opposition to the rhythm of wholeness, we will be off-balance. When we are moving away from the rhythm of belovedness, we will have a sense of disconnection. When we are moving apart from God's rhythm, we will not experience the joy of the dance.

In some ways, moving out of step with the rhythm of wholeness is easy. So many people are doing it right along with us. In other ways, it is a weary-making enterprise to move against what will give us life. When the idea for this book first flitted across the top of my mind—as ideas mysteriously seem to do—I had come to the realization that my exhaustion was not so much physical exhaustion but soul-level weariness. Rather than dance through my life, I tried to push, pull, and stomp my way toward whatever strange idea of success I was chasing. It turns out that it is exhausting to move against the rhythm that's intended for me. It's like trying to swim upstream or walk up a down escalator.

In an effort to listen for the rhythm that heals and restores, I looked at eleven different parts of daily life and examined the unique rhythm of holy and sacred days from my Christian faith. In these daily habits and moments—from how we do our shopping and how we handle our free time to the way we disconnect ourselves from our food and the way we avoid grief and loss—we face opportunities and pitfalls. Sometimes we may find it easy to step in time with the rhythm that brings life; other times we might feel hopelessly stuck in a hamster wheel we can't escape.

Our disconnect from the sacred pulses and rhythms of the world is wearing us out. Psychologists have proposed the idea of nature-deficit disorder as a possible cause for a range of behavioral problems in children. Richard Louv, author of *The Nature Principle: Reconnecting with Life in a Virtual Age*, writes, "The future will belong to the nature-smart—those individuals, families, businesses, and political leaders who develop a deeper understanding of nature and who balance the virtual with the real. . . . The more high-tech our lives become, the more nature we need to achieve natural balance." For Louv, the disconnect between people and nature has wide-ranging consequences. I believe those consequences are profound. One of the ways we encounter God is by spending time in the world God created, and we not only suffer physically, mentally, and emotionally when we are disconnected from the rhythm of the world; we also lose sight spiritually too. Technology is only one way we disconnect from the sacred pulse. But no matter how we choose to separate ourselves from it, the end result remains the same: we become weary and are in desperate need of restoration.

In this book, you won't find a list of simple steps to get things back on track. The more I have researched and reflected, the more convinced I have become that this is a journey unique to each of us. Just as members of an orchestra play different instruments with different parts, we will find ways to dance and move that are unique to us. But we will all be playing the same symphony. Even if our journeys are unique, the sacred pulse is the same. Within the pages of this book, we will explore roadblocks to these holy rhythms as well as ways to listen anew for the sacred pulse in our everyday moments.

When we find ourselves depleted and aching, holy rhythms are still all around us. When we are longing for another way, God's restoring shalom is reaching out to embrace us. The ache that we feel inside is there to remind us that we can reclaim the rhythm. It's there. It's beating. It's inviting us to dance. We do not have to do enough, accomplish all the right things, or prove we deserve it. All we need to do is listen. The song is there, being sung over us; we just need to retrain our ears to hear it.

PART I

THE DANCE OF TIME

1

DRUMBEAT OF TIME
The Holy Rhythm of the Day

I have a complicated relationship with time. On one hand, I see time as an opportunity. Each new day is twenty-four hours filled with endless chances and fresh possibilities to get things accomplished. When I wake up in the morning, I prepare myself to race against time. I make menus and to-do lists, schedule reminders on my phone, and pride myself on using every minute I can to get as much done as possible. After spending hours racing against the clock, I end my day with all of the things I didn't finish running through my mind. There is never enough time to get it all done.

On the other hand, I see time slipping through my fingertips. I set goals, but I waste time on Facebook instead. I hesitate to make a phone call to someone, and then it is too late. I blink, and my kids have grown up. The problem with racing against time is that you can never catch it. You can never pass it. You can never beat it. As the schedule keeper in my house, I often feel like I am one step behind time—because I am. The ticking of the clock reminds me that there is too much to do and not enough time to do it, and the ephemeral nature of time reminds me that I have very little control over any of it. Trying to maximize every opportune moment leaves me feeling anxious and depleted.

Sometimes I try to spin my wrestling with time in a positive way and say I'm a good time manager. But if I'm honest, time often does an impressive job of managing me. When I allow myself to be driven by the drumbeat of time, I measure the success of my days by how much work I get done. I work harder and throw myself into my tasks headfirst, crossing items off the to-do list. I push myself to finish one more thing or add one more commitment to my calendar because I want my day to count. Yet a life lived to the heartbeat of the ticking clock is a life immersed in disappointment and frustration. The to-do list can never be finished.

In Psalm 90, the psalmist grapples with the brevity of his life when he writes, "For all our days pass away under your wrath; our years come to an end like a sigh. The days of our life are seventy years, or perhaps eighty, if we are strong" (Psalm 90:9–10). The psalm writer's response to realizing the limits of his time is not to cram as much into those seventy or eighty years as he possibly can. Instead, he councils himself—and us—to pay attention to the number of days we have. The psalmist continues, "So teach us to count our days that we may gain a wise heart" (Psalm 90:12). The days we have been given were not intended to be stuffed to the brim; they were meant to be received as a gift, as opportune moments to gain a wise heart.

I wonder if Psalm 90:1 is the fruit of the psalmist counting his own days: "Lord, you have been our dwelling place in all generations." For the psalmist, gaining a wise heart begins with seeing the end. As Walter Brueggemann puts it, "The psalmist recognizes that human life is finite and limited. The psalmist does not know or want to know the exact number of allotted days but is fully honest about the existence of a limit." Recognizing that our lives have an end is the beginning of listening to the rhythm of time that restores rather than destroys.

When my husband and I were first married, we quickly realized that we marched to the rhythm of two different beats. We were in our pickup truck one afternoon driving to a birthday party when I started panicking that we were going to be late. We managed to hit every red light along the way, and we even had to stop at the railroad tracks for a commuter train. Jeff was calm and laid back about all the difficulties we encountered, as only a well-practiced Chicago driver could be. I was in the passenger seat taking deep breaths trying to calm myself down. We made it to the birthday party right on time, but I felt embarrassed as we walked up to the front door. Jeff softly reminded me that we weren't late, but I still felt stressed. I believed that if you weren't early, you were late.

As the oldest child in my family, I was responsible for checking in with my parents when my brother and I went anywhere by ourselves. We would go to the city swimming pool in the summer, and I would hide a quarter in my shoe so that I could use the pay phone if we needed to come home later than planned. I learned the importance of keeping a watchful eye on the clock, and I began to associate time management with being grown-up. I internalized the idea that effective time management is the gateway to responsibility. When you are in charge, you have to watch the clock. I began to see efficiency and time management as a way to prove to my parents, to my friends, and to others that I was dependable.

I began marching in step with *chronos* time.

As a first-semester seminary student, I was surprised to learn that there is more than one word in Koine Greek for "time." *Chronos*, the root of "chronological," is a word that refers generally to "time." *Chronos* is about sequence and quantity. By contrast, the word *kairos* refers to the fullness of time, an opportune moment. *Chronos* is the ticking timepiece, but *kairos* recognizes the sacredness of particular moments. As we seek to tap into the sacred pulse of the day, we must move beyond seeing time merely as a collection of minutes and hours to embracing its sacredness.

Jesus knew the importance of each moment. In John 7, Jesus's brothers urged him to show himself to the world (because they did not believe in him, as the Gospel writer put it), and Jesus responded, "My time has not yet come" (John 7:6). He understood *kairos* time. The time would come when the world would see who he was, but the time had not yet arrived. We receive opportunities every day to embrace and savor the time we have been given. When I cram my days so full I can hardly breathe or get sucked into scrolling on social media, I lose invaluable moments I can never get back. Deep down, I know this, but it is easy to convince myself that it is just a minute here or a minute there. The time that slips away may be made up of *kairos* moments: moments of opportunity, instances in which the sacred draws beautifully close to us. The sacred pulse of each day encourages us to move in step with these holy opportunities rather than with the driving force that urges us to maximize every second.

Many of the first Christians were Jews. Jewish Christians were accustomed to worshipping on the Sabbath—on Saturday—and after the resurrection, they continued going to the synagogue. These early Christians also began worshipping on Sunday—the first day of the week—to celebrate the resurrection and to have fellowship with each other as the body of Christ. These Sundays were sometimes referred to as the "eighth day" because the community was gathering as a part of the new creation God inaugurated in Jesus. The early church understood that time had been redefined in Jesus. Time was not merely a chronological collection of hours; time itself was being redeemed.

As people who long to reclaim God's rhythm for our lives, we are called to participate in this redemption process. Our moments are not mere moments; they are everything. "How we spend our days is, of course, how we spend our lives," Annie Dillard writes. "What we do with this hour, and that one, is what we are doing."

Blue Light and Daylight

Each morning when the sun rises, we receive a fresh opportunity to listen again for the sacred pulse of time. Yet many of us choose to begin each day with blue light rather than daylight. In one report, four out of five people admitted to looking at their smartphones within fifteen minutes of waking up. Of that four out of five, almost all of them said they look at their phones before they've done anything else for the day. Gone are the days when people first dragged themselves out of bed to brush their teeth or brew some coffee. Today many people reach over to the bedside table, grab their phones, and scroll on social media or email until the grogginess has worn off.

If this doesn't sound like such a big deal, perhaps some honesty is in order. For me, on the mornings when I grab my phone before I do anything else, time slips away quicker than I realize. The next thing I know, I should have been showered, dressed, and working on breakfast, but I am still in bed. Once I realize how much time I've squandered, the stress kicks in. I have wasted so much time that I am no longer able to accomplish everything that's needed before I head out the door for the morning. Sound familiar? If it does, you are not alone. The vast majority of smartphone owners are in the same boat—or bed—not getting ready for the day like they need to be.

In a very practical sense, we have distanced ourselves from the sacred pulse of time by relying on artificial lights rather than daylight. The invention of the light bulb meant that the rhythm of sunrise and sunset no longer dictated

the way people lived. The harnessing of light, the control-
ling of it outside of daylight hours, made incredible things
possible. When it became too dark to work in the field,
farmers could turn on their tractors' headlights. Bedside
lamps allowed students and readers to stay awake with
their books way past their bedtimes. Researchers have been
able to view and explore places that would have been out of
reach, like murky, deep ocean waters. We can drive places
at night, attend concerts and movies, and watch baseball
games after dark, all because we have light at our fingertips.

While many of these innovations have enriched our
lives, our reliance on these artificial lights disconnects us
from the natural rhythm of light and dark that our bodies
need. Our dependence on a different rhythm, which doesn't
have much rhyme or reason to it, is not only a disruption
to our bodies; it is physically unhealthy. Sleep scientist
Matthew Walker puts it this way: "Sadly, human beings
are in fact the only species that will deliberately deprive
themselves of sleep without legitimate gain." The invention
of the light bulb and other light-producing technologies
has enabled us to burn the candle at both ends.

I experience this tension between the rhythms of artificial light and daylight when I crochet. When working on
a crochet project, I find it difficult to put my work down.
I can work on a stuffed crochet creature until the sun has
set. When I first start crocheting, I position myself near a
window so the sunlight makes it easier for me to see each
stitch. Sometimes I don't want to quit working once it is too
dark to see, so I move upstairs and turn on a lamp. While
lamps have helped me meet many self-imposed deadlines

(like making gifts for my kids for Christmas), they have also enabled me to choose work over sleep. In the moment, I love being able to get more accomplished on my project, but I almost always regret it when I wake up exhausted the next morning.

Each of us has a master clock inside our brain that organizes the rhythm of our body's systems. This clock is located inside of the hypothalamus, and it receives its input from our eyes. The stimulation of light to our eyes outside of daylight hours can disrupt that clock, which can result in a host of chronic health conditions. Night shift workers are shown to be at a higher risk for gastrointestinal problems, heart disease, and even certain cancers, possibly because the body suppresses the release of melatonin when surrounded by lights during nighttime hours.

"The eye is the lamp of the body," Jesus said. "So, if your eye is healthy, your whole body will be full of light; but if your eye is unhealthy, your whole body will be full of darkness. If then the light in you is darkness, how great is the darkness!" (Matthew 6:22–23). Even though Jesus wasn't speaking of sleep health and biological clocks, his words ring true: what comes into our eyes affects not only our spiritual health but our physical health as well. The light that comes into our eyes changes the way our bodies function, which should give us pause as we consider the hours we spend in front of screens.

Many vital services need to be available around the clock for our communities to function. Sometimes absolutely nothing can be done about the disruption of our biological clocks (though those who work the night shift do often find ways to combat the negative effects on their health). But for many of us, the disruption of our biological clocks is a lifestyle choice. In Genesis 1, when God created the heavens and the earth, the first act of creation was the separation of light and darkness. This separation was about order and marking time, but it was also a demonstration of a rhythm that will give us life. The human body needs time to rest, to sleep, to be restored. We need a division between our waking, working life and our sleeping, restorative one.

Time Is Not about Me; It Is about Us

The creation of a worldwide, shared understanding of time was not about community but power. As Walter Brueggemann summarizes, "It is worth noting that the regulation of time in worldwide terms was accomplished in the service of the British navy, that is, in the service of power and control. [Carl] Honoré nicely observes, 'The telling time went hand in hand with telling people what to do.'" Rather than being rooted in bringing people together, the globalization of time was about labor and commodifying people. Scripture, however, offers a different view of time. This difference is a fundamental one that invites us to view one another as neighbors and friends rather than products for consumption.

In the book of Genesis, the pause of the seventh day was an equalizer. It did not matter whether you were a landowner or a servant, a man or a woman, wealthy or just surviving by the skin of your teeth: a time for rest was built into the fabric of life. As it says in the old song "John O'Dreams," "Both man and master in the night are one / All things are equal when the day is done." Sabbath rest was not to be dependent upon social status or merit; it was meant to be a balm for all.

Undergirding the understanding of time in the book of Genesis was the notion that everyone needed to stop moving, stop producing, stop being defined by the endless expectations and tasks of the daily grind. This is one reason Jesus made the radical statement, "The Sabbath was created for humans; humans weren't created for the Sabbath" (Mark 2:27 CEB). We were not created to serve time. We were created to be restored by time. All of us. The only time Jesus deviated from that Sabbath rhythm was in the service of others. He healed and restored people on the Sabbath because time was meant to be a gift to us, not a prison. Time is for knitting people together as a community, for recognizing the humanness of each other, and for working together in ways that mend and give life.

But how we love *chronos* time! When I was about to begin my first year of college, I received a survey in the mail that sought to pair me up with the right roommate. The survey included a few questions about time: Are you a night owl or an early riser? Are you a procrastinator, or do you work ahead on your assignments? Do you stay up late on the weekends or keep the same daily schedule? The questions intended to help connect us with people who perceived time in the same way we did, and I understand why. Someone who prefers to stay up late finishing assignments might struggle to share a living space with a person who goes to bed early and is up before the sun.

We define ourselves and others by the way we engage with time. Time can bring us together, but it is often used instead as a way to separate us into groups (or even into solitude) based on how we interact with *chronos* time. Time becomes about *me*, and what I can do within time's confines, rather than about *us*. The way I interact with time becomes a way of separating myself from community, of defining who I am and what I'm worth. Life lived to the beat of *chronos* time is no longer about how we can better be in community with each other. It becomes the driving force that pulls each of us in as many different directions as there are people and schedules. Life lived to the beat of *chronos* time becomes a life of separation, weariness, and discontent.

We are invited, instead, into a *kairos* way of life. The pulse of redeemed time is about sacred moments rather than efficiency. We move in step with the pulse of time not because we have something to prove but because we are already beloved, even before we have done anything at all. *Kairos* time is about counting our moments, recognizing they are fleeting, and allowing ourselves to dance in a way that transcends the confines of *chronos* time. Deadlines, meetings, and to-do lists will still exist, but the goalposts will have changed. In *kairos* time, we are no longer defined by what we accomplish but by the way we show the love of God in the moments we are given. Redeemed time is not about measuring up to a particular standard but about responding to our days with gratitude. Every day, every moment, is a gift. The sacred pulse of time is the heartbeat reassuring us that we are beloved, even if all we did was get out of bed in the morning. When we stop hustling to prove our worth, we may begin to notice opportunities to share that belovedness with others. We may find that sacred moments were already all around us; we were just too busy to see them.

Presence or Distraction

Listening for the sacred pulse of time is about presence rather than distraction. I have spent much of my life becoming an expert at rushing along with the pace of *chronos* time. Yet even when I desperately desired a change, it wasn't enough to tell myself to slow down. I had been moving in step with the ticking of the clock for enough years that I couldn't seem to get out of that rhythm. In Western society, we have adopted an expectation of productivity and constant availability that spills over into every aspect of our lives. We may feel expected to be doing something at all times—at work and at home. We are urged to gauge our success by how much we've produced. We even speak about our blogging and social media usage as "creating content." We set the bar high for getting things done but also create habits that distract us from the work we need to do. We have both busied ourselves to the brim and made it ridiculously difficult to get our work done. If this isn't a self-defeating way to struggle through life, I am not sure what is.

This chaotic pace of life retrains our brains. Remember that biological clock in our brains that helps us keep our bodies healthy? Hartmut Rosa, professor of sociology at Friedrich Schiller University Jena, examines the way technology, social change, and the pace of life work together to accelerate society. These changes sometimes create discord between our brain's understanding of time and the social expectations around time. Rosa says that "modern society can be understood as an 'acceleration society,'" a reality that exists because of "technical acceleration and an increase in the pace of life due to chronic shortage of time resources." In other words, technology is changing rapidly, which changes social expectations, and the consequence is that the pace of life speeds up.

Technology saves time, but that time-savings changes social and professional expectations. Because of technology, we are *able* to communicate with people all around the world, and because of technology, we are *expected* to communicate with people all around the world. The smartphone in my pocket allows me to check in with my work from almost anywhere, but it also conditions me to expect others to check in from almost anywhere. Even though technology creates innovative ways to save time on tasks, these technologies also change our expectations for how long each job should take. As technology shortens the amount of time tasks take, we are expected to accomplish more in less time. Is it any wonder we feel hopelessly behind?

These changes urge us to hyperfocus on *now*. We read extreme examples of this in the news. A driver hears the ping of a new text message and glances down to read it, only to drive into a lake. A tourist stands too close to the edge of a cliff to get a coveted selfie, only to fall over the edge. On a smaller scale, many of us prioritize instant digital connection rather than personal connection. Parents (myself included) choose to check Facebook notifications right as our children are getting out of school for the day. Even though my child has been away from home for seven hours and has many stories and experiences to share, the craving for instant digital connection compels me to look at my phone instead of connecting with my child in front of me. I often choose *now* over longer-lasting relationships.

When I realized how often I choose fleeting technological connection over being fully present to people around me, I knew I needed to make a change. I decided to leave my phone behind when I pick up my kids from school. We have also made our family dinner table a technology-free zone. Even though I fall back into bad habits sometimes, I notice that when I keep my phone out of reach, I am less tempted to choose screens over personal connection. Those real-time choices have long-term consequences, even as the technology at our fingertips encourages us not to think beyond the moment. We all know that we should choose people over our devices, but we can still feel compelled, perhaps by the spike in dopamine, to seek the instant gratification of a notification over building relationships and making memories. I often lack the self-control to put my phone down in those moments. I have to put it out of sight so that I don't miss out on the *kairos* moments all around me.

Embracing the sacred pulse of time is a difficult task in a world full of distractions. Stepping out of the chaotic rhythm of sleep deprivation and round-the-clock exposure to lights and screens is not a simple thing to do, even when we have committed ourselves to doing it. We first have to cut ourselves some slack and realize we are not just hopelessly terrible at setting boundaries: "Behind every screen on your phone, there are generally like literally a thousand engineers that have worked on this thing to try to make it maximally addicting," former Mozilla and Jawbone employee Aza Raskin told a journalist. Raskin developed the capability to scroll infinitely on an app, which means you can mindlessly scroll without ever having to stop. You never have to click on anything. The screen never needs to refresh. A constant stream of connection and information flows at your fingertips without you ever having to pause or reflect. "If you don't give your brain time to catch up with your impulses . . . you just keep scrolling," Raskin says. Raskin did not realize the addictive quality of infinite scrolling when he first developed it, but he has since felt guilty for the way this technology has hooked us. Infinite scrolling creates a Bermuda Triangle for time. We log on and entire hours disappear.

Listening for the Sacred Pulse of Time

Listening for the sacred pulse of time is a challenge in a world saturated with blue light. It is difficult because many of our jobs, our relationships, and our hobbies depend on screens and are built around expectations of constant productivity. The first step in listening for the sacred, restorative rhythm of the day is taking an inventory of how we are spending our time:

- How many hours do we spend in front of screens?
- How many of those hours are necessary?
- What are our time wasters—our Bermuda Triangles for time?
- Where are we choosing distraction over presence?

By identifying the apps or devices that make our time (and our lives) disappear, we can set about changing our habits. When we pinpoint the ways we prioritize distraction over relationships, we can begin to do the difficult work of setting things right again.

I have found that I live my life by blue light on way too many dark, early mornings, and far too many dark, late nights. This discovery has helped me create some boundaries. I allow myself a set amount of time with blue light prior to bedtime, and my phone no longer charges in my bedroom. Reconnecting with the rhythm of time means reattuning myself and my habits to the rising and setting of the sun.

Listening again to that sacred rhythm may mean sleeping more, resting more often, or putting work aside earlier. If I'm feeling especially tired on a dreary winter day, it may be that I need more sleep rather than more stimulation (by caffeine or screens). We may face pushback from others who are still marching in step with the productivity clock rather than their internal clocks. It won't be easy. A support system of at least one other person who will commit to making some of the same changes can help.

I have found that I make different choices when I'm not losing hours to blue light Bermuda Triangles. I tend to go to bed earlier. I start new habits, like reading a book before bed, instead of spending time on Instagram. At the end of a workday, I may opt to take a walk in the neighborhood instead of starting a new series on Netflix. The first thing I noticed when I decided to cut back on the time I spent on my phone was how much extra time I had. I had no idea how much time I wasted until I had those moments back with no screen vying for my attention. I got caught up on the dishes in the sink. I felt my anxiety lower. I laughed with my kids more.

Sadly, I gravitate back to screens and blue light even though I know how much better my life is when I set better boundaries in those areas. I have to show myself some grace as I realize just how much works against my willpower. Many people are invested in me spending as much time as possible online. Stepping back into the rhythm of time—allowing myself to be present for those *kairos* moments—has benefits I notice right away. It is amazing what rediscovering the rhythm God gave to us can do for our health and well-being.

In a society that prizes production over presence, the way we engage time will always be complicated. Yet the sacred pulse of time is always there, waiting for us to rediscover it. The recovering time-waster in me wants to try to rein myself back in by overscheduling and making more to-do lists, but usually, I need the opposite. Getting back in step with the rhythm of time means putting down the lists, the calendars, the phones, and the expectations so that we can take a look around and savor the moments and opportunities being given. Listening again to the sacred pulse of time means listening to God's voice calling us beloved and allowing ourselves to receive that belovedness in each and every *kairos* moment we are given.

2

SYMPHONY OF THE SEASONS

The Holy Rhythm of Gardening

A s soon as I was able to tell the difference between ripe strawberries and underripe ones, Grandma took me out to her tiered, raised-bed strawberry patch to help her pick them. She rewarded our work with something delicious, like her homemade strawberry shortcake. My mom and dad also kept a garden, and they filled it with the vegetables we most enjoyed eating in the summer: zucchinis, tomatoes, cucumbers, and green beans. In addition to the old standbys, they grew some things, like birdhouse gourds, as happy little experiments. Some of my earliest memories are of being asked to check the garden for zucchinis ready for eating. I remember my parents putting up corn for the winter and my grandma's vast canning cellar filled with anything you could imagine, including pickles and homemade ketchup. Summers were for yard work, trips to the swimming pool, corn on the cob, and getting our hands dirty in the garden.

Yet even with my early gardening experiences, I had a limited understanding of where my food came from. I expected a variety of fruits and vegetables at the grocery store all year round, not realizing much of this produce had to be imported for that to be possible. I knew apple season only came around once a year, but I also knew that if we wanted apples, we could buy them at the grocery store. Nearly every shopping list my mom made included carrots, celery, and onions, and we would go to the store knowing that they would be available. I did not grow up selecting food based on what was in season. If I had taken time to think about it, I would have said that grocery stores carried the food we needed every day and gardens were for fun.

A surprising number of people do not know where their food comes from. In one survey, about 7 percent of respondents who were asked where chocolate milk comes from selected "brown cows" as their response. According to the USDA, Americans report that their favorite fruit is oranges (in the form of orange juice, that is) and their favorite vegetable is potatoes (in the form of French fries or potato chips). A child in upper elementary school told one interviewer for an agricultural literacy study that her mother said bread comes from an animal, but she didn't know which one. So while we might be tempted to say that kids these days don't know about food, it is not that simple. Children are learning what little they know from their parents who are sharing what they think they know with their kids.

Even with my years of childhood experience pulling weeds, planting seeds, and picking tomatoes, I entered adulthood with a surface understanding of what it means to be connected to my food. The first time I tried to plant my own garden, I noticed color-coded pictures of the United States on the back of each seed packet. The different colors showed what month of the year the seeds could be planted depending on where you lived. I decided I was going to grow green beans, but when I planted the seeds, the squirrels promptly came and dug them up. I built a little fence around my garden patch and tried planting more seeds, but the squirrels just climbed the fence. I was no match for the tenacious squirrels in Michigan, and I did not manage to grow any green beans successfully that year. As silly as it sounds, that was the first time I realized growing food was *hard*. You can't just plant seeds and count on them growing. Not until that moment did I learn that the world is not always a hospitable place for gardens. And only in recent years have I learned how disconnected many of us are from the rhythms and pulse of the seasons.

Disconnected from the Land

In the early 1800s, close to 75 percent of all people in the American workforce were farmers or in agriculture-related careers. This trend changed markedly by the turn of the twentieth century, and between 1950 and 1990, the number of people engaged in the work of agriculture declined steadily. By 2019, just under 11 percent of the American labor force was in farming or agricultural work, with only 1.3 percent in direct, on-farm employment. As people moved away from farms and ranches and into offices, industrialized societies became disconnected from the rhythm of the land. On a broad scale, this exodus away from agricultural careers led to changes in the way food was grown, prepared, and distributed. On a household level, many foods that were once made daily from scratch became items to purchase already made. Today, many major grocery store chains carry produce of all kinds regardless of the season of the year. On the flip side, for many children and adults, produce—in season or otherwise—is not available in the grocery store at all. People who live in food deserts have become further removed from where food comes from not because of an abundance of choices but because of a scarcity of availability.

Only a few generations ago, most people relied on drying or canning food in large quantities in order to have fruits and vegetables available in the winter. Year-round availability of produce enables people to do other kinds of work besides growing their own food, but it also allows us to separate ourselves from the rhythm of the season in a way that carries with it some costs. We no longer experience the primal joy of seeing the first blossom on a plant, which brings the hope that fresh food will be available soon. We have lost the sense of urgency when rain doesn't fall for months and the soil is parched with thirst.

I won't romanticize homestead and farm work. Those were difficult and backbreaking days. Yet while we may be unable or unwilling to go back to the way things were generations ago, we must find a way to reconnect ourselves to the pulse and movement of the land where we live. And in so doing, we will find our way back to patience, joy, hope, and gratitude in ways we never expected. Whether we turn a large portion of our yards into gardens or tend to a few plants on our apartment balconies, moving in step with the sacred pulse of the seasons will transform us from consumers into participants.

Wendell Berry recognizes this when he writes, "Most eaters . . . think of food as an agricultural product, perhaps, but they do not think of themselves as participants in agriculture. They think of themselves as 'consumers.'" While the difference between consumer and participant might seem like a semantic one, the distinction is important. Berry continues, "For [consumers], then, food is pretty much an abstract idea—something they do not know or imagine—until it appears on the grocery shelf or on the table." When we do not participate in the rhythm of the seasons and the pulse of gardening, we do not grow in appreciation for the food we have. We do not consider the burden our food production systems place on those who are in poverty, workers who are paid unjustly, or people whose communities lack even basic access to produce regularly.

The answer to this disconnect is not a return to pre-industrialization days. For the vast majority of us, it is impossible or impractical to raise all of the food we need for survival. Instead, we are called to examine our habits and choose ways to reconnect to the rhythm of the place where we live. We may not be able to return to homesteading, but we can learn to engage the changing seasons, and we can tend to the small corner of the earth we inhabit in ways that are authentic to each of us. The farmer still watches the skies, prays for rain, and is limited by the growing conditions each year. But even if we never grow any of our own food, we, too, can tune our ears to the song of the land.

In the United States, we have separated ourselves from the rhythm of growing the food we eat. We water lawns that do not provide any food value but occupy more surface area than any other "irrigated crop" in the United States. We eat food because we are bored, not because it is what we need. Because we are out of step with the food that we eat, we are less appreciative of the food we do have. We waste more readily. Our food isn't something we've toiled over; it's replaceable. Beyond that, we aren't even sure what makes up some of the food we eat. How does quinoa grow? Where do avocados come from? Did you know eggs come in more colors than white? Even the blue ones are safe to eat.

Reconnecting to Patience

I waited years after my disastrous attempt at growing green beans before I tried growing a garden again. Inspired by pictures of asparagus spears pushing through the ground, I decided to grow asparagus. In the photographs, the asparagus spears looked like alien fingers reaching toward the sky. The locals told me I needed to get my garden planted before Memorial Day weekend for the best yield. If I waited longer than that, I would miss out on prime days for garden growth.

When it was almost planting time, I headed to a greenhouse with my husband, and I asked someone who worked there for an asparagus plant. The greenhouse employee handed me a large, fern-like bush in a pot. As I stood there holding the plastic container filled with wiry, green branches, I realized I had no idea what I was doing.

On the trip home, I examined the label on the side of the asparagus plant. *Asparagus spears can be harvested three or four years after planting.* Three of four *years?* I suddenly understood why a bunch of asparagus was going for almost five dollars a bundle at the grocery store. If I was going to have an asparagus harvest, I was going to be in this for the long haul.

I took my asparagus bush and planted it in my garden right next to the strawberry plants I had purchased. I soon learned that it was unwise to plant two aggressive plants right next to each other. I tended that asparagus plant all season—not that it takes much to tend a garden in central Iowa. Generally, the central part of Iowa receives enough rainfall each year for a garden's needs (the same cannot be said of western Nebraska, where I now live). The hardest part was keeping the weeds at bay.

The asparagus plant grew into a fluffy bush, which eventually became laden down with red berries. Once again, asparagus surprised me. I had never realized that asparagus plants made berries (though they are not to be eaten). Watching the plant was miraculous in every stage. The rabbits enjoyed hiding underneath the furry fronds. The birds would land nearby and rest in its shade. Even though we weren't getting anything to eat from it, I found joy in watching my plant grow. That summer was filled with anticipation as we looked forward to enjoying the harvest.

The following spring, spindly asparagus spears began emerging from the soil. They looked like roots that were growing upside down. I spent another growing season watching the plant grow. We got a couple of strawberries to eat that year, but only a couple. The asparagus went to seed and produced an even larger bush than the year before. It was so heavy that some of the branches collapsed and sprawled across the ground.

Around that time, someone in town noticed the asparagus bush and asked why I was growing my own. I learned that if I just drove a couple miles south and then a couple miles east, I could get all I wanted growing wild in the ditch.

Evidently, wild asparagus is a thing in Iowa.

The third spring, the asparagus spears were about as big around as my little finger. My husband and I sneaked a couple of them to taste because we couldn't wait any longer. They were delicious, but two asparagus spears hardly make a snack. By the fourth year, we had asparagus growing reliably, and we looked forward to it every spring after that.

We had planted the asparagus with no idea how long we would live in our home or how many years we would be able to enjoy it. We planted it without realizing the patience it would require. But when we finally had enough asparagus growing that we could pair it with a summer meal, there was no way we were going to allow those tender, long-sought-after spears to go to the crisper drawer to be forgotten until they rotted. We savored each one.

There is something meaningful about tending to a garden for years without receiving any of the fruit of your labor. Jesus told a parable about a man who planted a fig tree. After three years, the tree still had not produced any fruit, and the man who planted it was beginning to see it as a waste of good soil. Why take up precious land with something that provides no benefit? But the gardener knew that sometimes these things take more time than we want to give them. The gardener responded, "Sir, let it alone for one more year, until I dig around it and put manure on it. If it bears fruit next year, well and good; but if not, you can cut it down" (Luke 13:8–9).

In this story, Jesus was referencing a passage from Leviticus 19 that commanded those who planted fruit-bearing trees to refrain from harvesting until the fifth year. For three years the fruit was off-limits. The fourth year the harvest was for the Lord. The fifth year the people could eat from those trees. The passage from Leviticus said that when people observed these customs, the harvest from the fruit trees "may be increased for [them]" (Leviticus 19:25).

As an avid hobby gardener, I have experienced the truth of this statement. I could have harvested all my asparagus spears the second year after planting them. They would have been safe to eat. But I also would have had no asparagus come up the next year—or at most, just a few. The practice of gardening has been fertile soil for new realizations and understanding. I have discovered both the beauty of depending on the pulse of the seasons and the discipline of waiting until things are ready. I still struggle with impatience, but I have learned in my garden that many things are worth the wait.

Reconnecting to Joy and Hope

When the day came for us to load up the moving truck and leave the home where we'd not only planted our asparagus but also raised our kids through their earliest milestones, I looked at my garden with sadness. We had poured eight years into our ministry, our community, and our garden. We had gone from watching our strawberry plants grow to harvesting gallons of berries every summer and from waiting impatiently to taste homegrown asparagus to enjoying it every year. As we left, I said to my husband, "I hope the person who comes after us will get as much joy out of these plants as we have." But I knew they wouldn't.

Even if the people who lived there after us loved the harvest, they had not experienced the struggle of getting new plants to grow. They had not waited with anticipation for the first taste. Something about the hours I had spent with those plants made the produce that much sweeter. This realization made the expression "you are what you eat" mean something different to me. I poured myself into those plants. Partaking of them somehow completed a circle, filling up in me what had been poured out. I wasn't merely a consumer; I was somehow part of something larger than myself. I was a participant in the tilling and the keeping of the earth.

We moved to Nebraska in August of that year, and I remember feeling both excited for a new adventure and grieved over the things we were leaving behind. For the first spring in years, I wouldn't have any garden plants to look forward to. The first weeks after the move were busy as we transitioned to a new ministry and a new community and helped our kids get situated in a new school. Our hearts were full with all the new life and possibilities, but I still grieved that there would be no asparagus in the spring.

I decided that I needed to start planning for a future garden. I had learned many things from my first garden that would help me make my new garden better (like maybe *not* putting my asparagus and strawberry plants right next to each other). I ordered a seed catalog online and promptly forgot about it.

A few weeks later, I was lamenting the end of summer when the mail arrived. I walked out to the mailbox and retrieved the rolled-up magazine that had been placed inside. When I got back in the house, I unrolled it and saw a cover filled with pictures of joyous flowers and brilliantly colored fruits and vegetables. It was the catalog I had ordered. I flipped the booklet open, and the page I turned to had a bold advertisement that read, "It's not too late to plant garlic." It's *not*?

With winter on the horizon, it seemed impossible to me that it was the right time to plant anything. But perhaps it wasn't too late to plant seeds of spring hope. Perhaps there was still time to have something to look forward to. I did some research, and it turns out garlic is planted in the fall. In fact, many gardening resources recommend planting garlic after the first light frost. I looked through all of the varieties of garlic in the seed catalog, amazed. I'd only ever seen one kind of garlic at the grocery store. I decided upon Samarkand garlic, mostly because the catalog was running a special where you could buy one pound of "irregulars" for a deeply discounted price. I love garden plants, and I also love a good bargain.

Garlic irregulars are heads of garlic that have slightly fewer cloves in them than what is optimal for their variety. I decided that since I had never grown garlic before, there was no need to be picky. I ordered my pound of garlic irregulars in the middle of September knowing that, once they arrived, I would need to get them in the ground right away. What I didn't know was that one pound of irregulars was way more garlic than I needed. Most of the garlic I received wasn't even irregular. Each had a full ten to twelve cloves per head. Each head of garlic was like a beautifully wrapped package, just like the ones in the catalog.

We planted thirty-nine cloves of garlic that season (with a whole lot of irregulars leftover) and covered over what we had planted with a mound of grass clippings. It felt strange to plant something with snow in the forecast, but we decided to trust the research and give it a try.

Throughout the winter, I thought about the garlic we had planted. Could it really survive the harsh cold and snow? One January day, I went outside to take out the trash, and I glanced over into my garden on the way into the alley. I noticed something green in the garlic patch but thought it seemed unlikely anything had started growing yet. I quickly finished taking out the garbage and went into my garden to get a closer look. Sure enough, green plants were push-ing up through the snow. Wait, what? My mind raced with worry. What if the garlic had come up too early? What if the snow killed the plants? Aren't plants supposed to know when it is time to grow?

It turns out *that's what garlic does*. Garlic has a long growing season and needs to be planted in the fall for optimal growth. There is something about the cold and snow that enhances the garlic's flavor. The green sprouts that break through the ground may even freeze, but if that happens, new growth will develop when the temperatures warm up. All through the winter, I watched the garden for more signs of life. It might make me a garden nerd, but I found it inspiring to know that winter doesn't kill everything. Garlic is up to the task.

In the spring, I watched as the cloves of garlic grew into tall plants. In June, I marveled at the thick, curlicue stalks emerging from the middle of the plant. Each stalk was like an arrow directing you to make a U-turn. Once again, I ran to Google, where I discovered that these are called scapes. Not only are these unruly stalks fun to look at—they're also edible. My garlic plants had not only survived the winter; they were also growing a bonus crop—scapes that could be made into pesto or add some heat to a stir fry. Garlic was securing its place as my new favorite plant to grow.

That July, I harvested thirty-nine gorgeous heads of garlic. We bundled the garlic with twine and hung it in bunches to cure in the garage. Weeks later, we shared some with friends and family. We saved a few of the largest heads to plant in the fall. We tightly bundled the garlic we had left and used it through the winter. The flavor of fresh garlic was bolder and fresher than any garlic I had eaten before. The garlic cloves popped quickly and neatly out of the peels at first, but as they dried, they became stickier and harder to peel, more like garlic you can buy at the grocery store. I started to wonder how old the garlic in the grocery store was. If my garlic was fresher four months after harvest, how long had the garlic on the shelf been in storage, in transit, or for sale?

I loved growing the garlic so much that I experimented with letting the garlic go to seed, and the next year I planted garlic seeds (in addition to garlic cloves). From seed to full head of garlic, the process takes three or four years to complete. It was a fun experiment. I prefer to grow my garlic from cloves, but it was valuable to me to learn the life cycle of the garlic plant.

The tenacity of garlic brought me hope and joy during a season when I desperately needed it. When the snow fell that first Nebraska winter and awakened the grief in my heart about leaving our Iowa home and garden, the garlic shoots emerging in the snow gave me the courage to allow myself to grow in a new place too. The planted cloves buried deep beneath the blanket of cut grass reminded me that death precedes resurrection. I needed to experience the grief of asparagus left behind, of letting go of beautiful people as we moved from one place to another, before I could experience the joy of new life and new beginnings.

Growing garlic taught me the importance of being rooted—not just where you live, but in the rhythms and pulse of the seasons of your life. In reconnecting to the land,

and to hope, joy, and patience, our eyes will be opened to the ways we are connected to one another and to the story that binds us all together. Nothing can live unless it first dies. And when it dies, it will grow and produce something more abundant than it had before.

More Than Consumers

When we separate ourselves from the rhythm of growing our own food, our connection to food becomes a consumer-product relationship. After spending nine months growing garlic and several weeks curing it for winter storage, I couldn't imagine throwing garlic away because I didn't get around to using it. Something I had given so much of myself to was something to be cherished, savored, and stewarded. In fact, as soon as I discovered the first clove of garlic starting to sprout at the end of the winter, I peeled every single remaining clove of garlic, minced, and froze them. It took me hours, and my hands smelled like garlic for days, but I wasn't about to throw it all in the trash.

We are meant to be more than consumers. When we reconnect to the rhythm of the seasons and become participants in the raising of our food, we will experience unexpected gifts. Even as our occupations have become increasingly specialized and technologized and we are unable to make a full return to growing all the food we eat, there are still many ways for us to reengage with the sacred pulse of gardening. One of the simplest ways to become participants is to ask questions about food. Ask the produce person at the grocery store which fruits and vegetables are in season. Allow yourself to wonder if there are varieties of carrots or potatoes or beans that you have never tried before. The simple act of asking helps us remember that food does not merely appear on the grocery store shelves. Our food had a process and a journey before it made its way to us.

Connecting to the sacred pulse of gardening means we have to be willing to get our hands dirty, literally. We need to crouch down and pull the weeds in the sidewalk cracks and feel the soil between our fingers (if not in a garden, in a plant pot on the windowsill). Perhaps we can't grow everything we need, but reconnecting with the growing of our food in small ways will revolutionize the way we connect with food daily. Even if all you have is a small back patio or balcony, try growing a small herb garden, or plant a tomato plant in a pot. Participate in the cycle of growing your own food in whatever way you possibly can. Find someone who has a garden and see if you might be able to help or, if growing plants is not your thing, consider visiting a local farmers' market or participating in community-supported agriculture (CSA), where you can connect with local farmers and purchase produce directly from them. Gardening has taught me not only the importance of reconnecting to the seasons but also that I cannot do it all on my own. I enjoy growing garlic but have not done as well with tomatoes. I share garlic with a friend, and she shares tomatoes with me.

As we listen once again to the sacred pulse of the seasons, we will be growing more than tomatoes, cucumbers, and onions; we will also be growing appreciation, joy, and delight. We will experience a depth of gratitude we may have never felt before as we sit down to the table—whether we are by ourselves, with friends, or with family—and enjoy food as participants. We'll appreciate each bite more deeply—and it might taste better too.

The blooms of springtime promise walks in the park and cookouts on the lawn, but they also call out to us that a new season of hope has begun. When people relied solely on the land, the sight of new spring growth was a harbinger of promise, a celebration of having survived another winter. The new flowers of spring still bring joy for those of us who find ourselves disconnected from the pulse of the seasons, but they do not as urgently remind us that we *lived*. Our modernized life may have changed the way our food is produced, but it does not have to separate us from it. We can choose to dig in and take part once again—participants in the tilling and the keeping of the earth.

3

CADENCE OF
THE KITCHEN
The Holy Rhythm of Mealtime

I was a clarinetist in concert band, but I disliked marching with my instrument enough that I asked my teacher if I could do *anything* else during marching season. For a couple of years, I was part of the color guard team, and then I switched to the marching bells (think xylophone that you carry on a harness fitted over your shoulders). The drum major would turn and face the band. She would raise her arms and blow four sharp notes on her whistle, and the percussion section would pick up her beat and continue it for the rest of the band to follow. If they rushed ahead, the band would too. If they lagged behind, the whole band would follow suit. In between marching band pieces, the percussion section played a cadence, a beat intended to keep the band marching in step in between songs. During those in-between moments, the cadence was everything. Without the cadence, the band would have no unifying beat to keep them moving together.

Mealtime is the cadence of our days, and we step in time with its beat. Each morning, we awaken and receive the opportunity to listen for the faint, distant call that urges us to orient our pace around its rhythm. Three times a day—or twice for breakfast-skippers—we feed our bodies. We do this in many different ways: from picking up meals prepared by someone else to spending hours around beautifully spread tables with extended family or dear friends. We eat fast food and slow food. We savor comfort foods that remind us of childhood, and we step outside the box to experiment with new foods as we learn about them. Meals serve as touchpoints throughout our days, opportunities to check in with ourselves and listen again for the beat. We even talk about our lives in terms of food. We take working lunches and chat over coffee. We make promises to be home for dinner, even on the busiest of days.

For much of my adult life, even though I enjoy cooking and preparing meals, I have eaten a lot of convenience food because I thought the pace of my life demanded it. I believed that I had little choice in the matter. Living a busy life meant having to make sacrifices, and often the first routine on the chopping block was making home-cooked food. Yet the longer I was in this habit of feeding myself whatever was fastest (rather than what nourished my body and spirit), the more I recognized my need for change. Mealtime isn't about giving our bodies just enough energy to keep going. It's about listening for the cadence that brings us life and joy and allowing ourselves to fall in step with its rhythm. Every time we pause to feed our bodies, we are invited to listen again for the beat. As we listen, we are urged to allow the rhythm to take up residence in our lives so that its movement becomes instinctive.

The beat of our mealtime cadence is love—love for ourselves and love for our neighbors. The rhythm of our meals is not about the kind of food that graces our tables or the amount of time or skill that went into preparing our meals—though these things can certainly help. Instead, the way we pull up our seats and gather to eat provides us with an opportunity to live into the two great commandments that Jesus gave to his disciples—and to us—so many years ago: to love God and to love our neighbors as we love ourselves (Matthew 22:34–40). The many tables we gather around over the course of our lives, different though they may be, offer us places where we can experience nourishment, relationships, belonging, and love. When we have fallen out of step with the cadence and rhythm, we may find these tables instead to be places where we experience the opposite: longing, brokenness, exclusion, and disconnection. We may come to the table hungry for belonging and relationship, and we might leave hungrier than when we first came.

We Belong at the Table

Eating is intimate. It is a primal, basic, and necessary activity as we care for the bodies we have been given. When we eat, we are vulnerable. Just as Jesus was made known in the breaking of the bread to the disciples he encountered on the road to Emmaus, so too are we made known to ourselves and to others as we eat (Luke 24:28–35).

We often acknowledge that eating with others is an intimate thing, but we do not always recognize the intimacy of eating by ourselves. When we eat alone, we can explore our thoughts, our hearts, our hopes, our dreams, and our very selves. At the table, in a unique way, we become authentic to ourselves. In the space of a quiet meal, we may be confronted with the emotions of a difficult day. We may find inspiration as we experience and savor a delicious dish. The act of doing something basic and repetitive opens us up to discover who we are. For this reason, meals in solitude can be a gift, though they can also be difficult as we experience feelings of loneliness and exclusion.

When we eat with others, our vulnerability meets the vulnerability of those around our shared table. As we eat together, it is as though we are planting seeds in each other's hearts. We might find ourselves amazed as we become rooted together around the food we share.

When you ask people about their fondest memories from childhood, you'll find they often revolve around food. At Thanksgiving, my grandma always made extra homemade rolls because she knew how much I loved them. My great-aunt always brought sweet celery because we couldn't have Thanksgiving without it. After a miles-long day of backpacking in the mountains when I was a preteen, the spaghetti we cooked over a campfire—complete with the "extra protein" of the mosquitoes that got too close—tasted better than any spaghetti I had ever had before. The bonds formed around those meals and around those tables (even the invisible table of the campfire) strengthened our relationships, fed our bodies, and nourished our spirits. Our meals reorient us, connect us, and remind us of who we are. They are daily opportunities to be refreshed, recalibrated, and restored. They are invitations to share what's inside our hearts with ourselves and with those who are close to us.

Henri Nouwen recognized the opportunity for loving ourselves and our neighbors at the table: "Isn't a meal together the most beautiful expression of our desire to be given to each other in our brokenness?" Nouwen writes. "The table, the food, the drinks, the words, the stories: Are they not the most intimate ways in which we not only express the desire to give our lives to each other, but also to do this in actuality? I very much like the expression 'breaking bread together,' because there the breaking and the giving are so clearly one." As we share food around the table, we share our very selves. We invite others to experience us in our humanness, and we give each other the gift of presence. We listen and are listened to, we give and receive, we know and are known.

Far too often, however, our experiences around tables are not experiences of love. Sometimes we come to the table after a conflict, and the tensions remain high. Each plate passed and every deep breath exhaled is a painful reminder of the distance that separates. Other times, we may not experience outright conflict and tension around the table, but distractions keep us from connecting with one another or even with ourselves. Consciously or not, we may fear the intimacy of our tables and turn on the television or check our phones so that we won't have to talk to each other. We may eat in our cubicle to avoid feeling the isolation of the break room. Or we may skip meals here or there because we become immersed in our work, the regular rhythm of which trains us *not* to show love for our bodies in the way Christ loved us. We fall into the rhythm of eating for survival rather than orienting our lives around the cadence of love's table.

Jesus at the Table

Jesus knew the power of sharing meals, and he chose to eat them with the most unlikely of people. The religious authorities did not approve. Luke records their complaint this way: "And the Pharisees and the scribes were grumbling and saying, 'This fellow welcomes sinners and eats with them'" (Luke 15:2). Throughout Jesus's life, he prioritized people, and he showed them love by eating with them. The leaders of the day were not scandalized by the fact that Jesus ate with other people; hospitality and meal-sharing were expected in Jesus's day. What ruffled feathers and raised eyebrows was that Jesus sat around tables with people of questionable reputation and occupation. By sitting with those the world shamed, Jesus put himself in a position to be a recipient of that same shame.

Jesus did not expect people to change their lives before he ate with them. When Jesus called Levi the tax collector to follow him, Levi threw Jesus a banquet, and they ate together. The issue was not so much that Jesus called Levi to follow him but that Jesus was willing to share a meal with Levi before Levi had done anything to change his reputation. In another mealtime setting, Jesus taught the guests that they should not invite their friends, relatives, or wealthy neighbors to share meals with them. Instead, Jesus urged, we ought to invite those who would be unable to pay us back.

Meals to Jesus were not about status; they were about gathering to share and receive the love of God. Who most needs that love? Perhaps it wasn't those who were working the hardest to be close to God but those who hadn't even been allowed to try. Ultimately, Jesus shared a final meal with his friends—a ragtag group that, despite their differences, had Jesus in common. He told them to share the same meal with one another and remember him until he came again.

Jesus shared meals with people because something happens when we eat together. We are not merely sharing food; we are sharing ourselves. When we eat together, we offer each other who we are, quirks and all. We are united as humans, each of us needing to pause and eat no matter our social status or background. As we eat together, we might experience a union that transcends whatever divides us from each other.

When I was a sophomore in high school, I moved to a new state. For the first several months at my new school, I would go into the cafeteria, buy something a la carte, and find a secluded place to sit in the commons. I chose to eat by myself rather than experience the isolation of not being invited to sit at someone else's table. I chose loneliness over rejection. When you have experienced exclusion, isolation, or rejection, those painful moments stick with you. Rather than allow myself the possibility of being hurt, I closed myself off to invitation. A quiet, lonely lunch was safer than being turned away.

I imagine the wonder and surprise of Jesus's listeners as he told them parables comparing the kingdom of God to a banquet and a wedding feast. The guests at the feasts were the outcasts, those who had lived lives of rejection and isolation. Contrary to the tables of this world, Jesus's table welcomes those who are typically excluded and honors those who have been shamed. The guest list includes the marginalized, the unexpected, the forgotten, and the outcast. Jesus knew that meals are places of sharing. They are places of give-and-take. Each mealtime is not only an opportunity to meet our physical need to be fed; it is a place to be nourished in body and spirit. When Jesus shared meals with others, he invited them to share in his love and welcome. His welcome transformed hearts and lives. By sharing a table with Jesus, all who gathered had the opportunity to taste—quite literally—the kingdom of God and participate in the feast of love that transforms and nourishes.

In the ancient world, honor was seen as a limited commodity. If you received honor, someone else had to receive shame; there simply was not enough honor to go around. People criticized Jesus for eating with people who were viewed as shameful and for allowing their shame to become his own shame. Jesus showed instead that honor, love, and welcome are not limited goods. By sharing tables with those who had typically been marginalized, Jesus showed that we do not have to push others down in order to lift ourselves up. We are not made holy by declaring others unholy. We are not loved when others are unloved. Around Jesus's table, all are welcome, even those who have been declared unwelcome by this world. Perhaps especially them.

Over the course of my adult life, I have set many tables for myself that were not places of nourishment and refreshment. Even when I worked hard to prioritize home-cooked meals, I found myself exhausted and over-whelmed. Too many times tables have been places where I smoldered with resentment about all of the work I needed to do or all of the tasks that didn't get accomplished that day. Far too many tables have been places where I excluded myself from others, and even from my deepest self. I have come to realize that while certain approaches to mealtime may lend themselves more easily to love and nourishment and relationship, no one practice works in and of itself. Eating at home can be the most isolating experience while eating takeout food in the front seat of the car can be the seedbed of welcome and gratitude.

When our children were little, we endeavored to keep a routine of eating our evening meals at home. I imagined that many families were no longer keeping this home-based mealtime ritual, and I prided myself that we were some-how hanging on to this piece of the "good old days." I was surprised when I read the results of a 2017 report called "The Future of Dinner" that revealed that 80 percent of all dinners in the United States are eaten at home. Yes, more of those meals contained prepackaged ingredients than what our parents or grandparents used, but meals were still being eaten at home the vast majority of the time. The report claimed that if trends continued in the same way, even more people would be eating at home in the future. Even as access to already-made foods is on the rise, people still prioritize eating at home.

And yet, at the same time as this report was issued, former US Surgeon General Vivek Murthy identified lone-liness as a silent health crisis in the United States. As Mur-thy explored the various health concerns surfacing in the United States during his time as surgeon general—such as opioid addiction and rates of heart disease and diabetes—he was surprised to encounter loneliness too. He writes, "But one recurring topic was different. It wasn't a frontline com-plaint. It wasn't even identified directly as a health ailment. Loneliness ran like a dark thread through many of the more obvious issues that people brought to my attention, like addiction, violence, anxiety, and depression." Perhaps the answer to reclaiming the rhythm of mealtime's love and welcome is not found only when we eat our meals at home. Despite the rise of meals at home, rates of loneliness have also steadily increased. So home-cooked meals don't necessarily correlate with a greater sense of belonging. Does that mean they don't matter at all?

Practicing Love and Belonging at the Table

I wonder if, despite the way many of us guard the need for being physically present at evening meals, we have neglected to guard the importance of mental and emotional presence. Many of us struggle to be fully present to the people around us (and to ourselves) when we gather for mealtime. This is something that I am working on, as I try to model for my children the kind of presence, attention, and empathy I hope they will show to others as they grow. I have to admit that, far too often, I allow my troubles to distract me. Often, the scapegoat is digital distraction—television, cell phones, or other things—and these are real distractions. But more often than that, I am distracted by the endless list in my mind: the dishes that will need to be washed once the meal is over, how busy the next day might be, what someone said to me earlier in the day.

At the table where Jesus instituted the last supper, the disciples shared broken and divided bread with Jesus. But they were not in want of his full presence. At that table of misfits, Jesus, the carpenter's son-turned-religious-teacher, shared bread with fishermen, a tax collector, a Zealot, and others. The last experience he shared with his friends was a meal. And he told them to remember him by celebrating this meal after he was gone. In her breathtaking book *Liturgy of the Ordinary*, Tish Harrison Warren writes, "At the Last Supper Jesus tells his disciples to eat in remembrance of him. Of all the things he could've chosen to be done 'in remembrance' of him, Jesus chose a meal." In the ordinariness of mealtime, Jesus chose to share the extraordinariness of his love. He took the bread, and he broke it, he blessed it, and he gave it to them. And as he did so, he offered them his very self. He did this for the disciples around the table, and he did it for every person who came after him who shared this meal in his name. He even did this for Judas, knowing that Judas's presence was divided, scattered, and caught up in the betrayal about to happen.

In the giving of the bread and the sharing of the cup, Jesus gave and shared himself in the ultimate act of presence. Jill J. Duffield puts it this way:

> We eat from the one loaf and drink from the one cup, reminding us that we are one in and through Christ Jesus our Lord. When we gather at the Table of the Lord, our relationship with Christ dictates our relationships with each other. United in Christ, we look back and remember the life, death, and resurrection of our Lord, and we anticipate his coming again. That anticipation calls for readiness to meet him face-to-face at any moment. Not drunk and divided, fractured and fatigued, but unified in love, outdoing one another in service, rejoicing that in Christ there is no longer Jew nor Greek, slave nor free, male nor female, but Christ is all in all.

Jesus showed the healing power of presence without qualification or distraction. In his attentive welcome, even those most ostracized and alone found a home.

The last supper—and every gathering around the Lord's table since—is a place of presence, nourishment, and love.

In some small way, every table we gather around has the potential to share little glimpses of these gifts too. We may be sharing a meal that took all day to prepare, or we may be heating up a frozen pizza after a long and tiring day; regardless, each mealtime is a moment to practice offering the gift of presence to ourselves and others. When we eat, we have the opportunity to listen, pay attention, and slow down. You know the truism that we have two ears and only one mouth because we are supposed to be twice as quick to listen as we are to speak? When my mouth is busy eating, I'm twice as likely to listen.

When I fall out of the rhythm of mealtime's cadence, I miss out on the love and relationship that refresh my spirit. When I bring my divided and scattered self to the table and I do not pause to experience the nourishment of presence, I leave the table with a full stomach but an empty heart. Mealtimes were never meant to be an item on the day's to-do list. Rather, the rhythm and the cadence have always been driven by love. How wonderful that we are invited to have this experience throughout our days. In the ordinariness of our meals, and in the extraordinariness of the Lord's Supper, we can practice being present. At the Lord's table, I experience the undivided presence of Christ so that I might be nourished and experience the love of God's presence. I learn anew how to be present to myself and others.

I am still struggling to hear the far-off beat of this cadence. I approach far too many meals as a divided person who longs to be present but manages to keep myself from doing so. I do not have all the answers. But I do know that presence often begins by reading the room. Where are the distractions? What threatens to separate me from those sharing my table and from my own thoughts? Am I regularly bringing the troubles of work home? What distractions am I setting up as barriers between myself and others?

The struggle to be present encourages us to consider what obstacles might be getting in the way. Sometimes the problem requires a simple solution, like everyone leaving their electronic devices in a basket so that mealtime is a distraction-free zone. Other times our habits lead us to discover painful truths, like fears of allowing others to know who we are or hurtful memories of dysfunctional situations. The way to discover mealtime's cadence of love may be as varied as each of us are, but the process begins with a willingness to pay attention.

In my church, we cultivate the practice of being present to ourselves and each other whenever we pray the prayer of confession. During the prayer of confession, we have a prayer that we all pray out loud together, but we also allow a full minute of silence as we confess our sins individually. The first time I experienced this minute-long silent prayer, I squirmed in my seat. I worried that my kids were chattering too much, and I wondered if the speaker leading the prayer time hadn't realized how much time had passed. The longer I have participated in this weekly ritual, however, the more I have come to appreciate it as a way of coming back to myself. We spend so much of our lives surrounded by noises and expectations that we forget to cultivate moments of quiet where we can listen. These same noises are often present in our lives and in our hearts regularly, and mealtime is an opportunity to slow down long enough so that we can listen to what is being whispered.

The evening meal when I was growing up was the center we returned to every day. No matter how busy our schedules became, my brother and I were expected to find our way back to the dinner table. Even though times are different, and the pace of life has changed, mealtimes remain a constant opportunity to reorient ourselves around the cadence's beat. We gather at the table to be fed in both body and spirit, and we gather at the table to be present to ourselves, to others, and to the God who loves us.

Jesus was made known all those years ago in the breaking of the bread, and Jesus continues to be known to us in the broken bread at the communion table and in the sharing of the bread around our many tables. As we gather to eat, we can listen to the faint whisper calling us back to ourselves. We can believe the voice telling us we are God's beloved. This is mealtime's pulse. It is not about our culinary skill, the table's presentation, or the number of people who gather to share with us. Mealtime is an opportunity to reconnect with ourselves and with others and to marvel in the belovedness God has given to each of us. Around the table, we are invited to experience the love of God.

PART II

THE DANCE OF
INTENTIONALITY

4

TEMPO OF TRANSACTIONS
The Holy Rhythm of Shopping

One of the first things my husband and I tried to find after we moved to Nebraska was a good coffee shop. Right on the main street of our new town, we discovered an airy, vibrant place with such good coffee and service we decided to go back a few days later. On our second visit, I hadn't even pushed the front door open all the way when the barista called out to us in a friendly voice, "Jeff and April, it's so good to see you this morning!" I stopped in my tracks hearing my name from someone who had only seen me once before. I hadn't realized until that moment that my biggest fear in moving to a larger community was the fear of being unknown. In the smaller town we had moved from, we knew people and people knew us. Each trip to the post office in that small town was sprinkled with friendly words and familiar faces. Every visit to the grocery store included conversations with the people behind the meat counter and at the checkout. And yet on this second coffee shop visit in our new town, someone had made the effort to know me. She knew my name, and she grew over time to know my regular drink order. She even shared a book with me she thought I'd like. "Don't feel like you have to rush to return it," she said. "It's OK if it takes you two years to get it back to me."

I love coffee shops because they push back against the consumer impulse in Western society. In a world that tries to make shopping efficient, quick, and cheap, coffee shops invite us to come in, sit a while, and get to know the people around us. Even though I drink a lot less caffeine than I used to, I still long for mornings in a coffee shop surrounded by people who are talking, being creative, studying, and sharing with others.

Shopping is an inconvenient task marketed in a prettied-up, convenient package. But rather than embracing the inefficiency of buying things, our consumer culture has tried to push shopping to become a user-friendly experience. Online shopping boasts "buy it now" options and nearly overnight shipping. In-person stores have added apps, rewards cards, and discounts for store-specific credit cards as a way to entice buyers to focus on the benefits of shopping rather than on what's lost. In many stores, self-checkout lines have almost entirely replaced checkout lines where you interact with a person. The main goal of these additions is to convince the shopper that the perks and efficiency offered are enough to counter any disruption shopping might cause.

When I default to buying things online or at big-box stores, it's mostly for the sake of convenience. Sometimes I shop online or at large retailers due to a lack of local availability. Sometimes I rely on online shopping for reasons of practicality and necessity. Online shopping filled a needed role during the pandemic as we avoided public spaces for reasons of health and safety. Even without a global health crisis, online shopping meets needs for many folks who are unable to shop in person. Online shopping has its place, and for many, it is an essential way to buy items.

But let's face it: many of us choose it just for convenience. You can look for an item from the comfort of your own home. You can price shop and compare without ever having to talk to anyone. You can find the item for a steal and receive it in a quick turnaround time. And you can do it all at 11:30 p.m. in your pajamas and fuzzy slippers. When I choose to shop this way, it is because it benefits me personally, and online marketplaces cater to that.

The word *convenience* comes from the Latin word *convenire*, which means "to come together." Convenience happens when things come together in a helpful way. Convenience meets certain desires and expectations that benefit us in the immediate. Online shopping offers benefits that make local shopping seem inconvenient. These convenience retailers gain business by promising consumers the opportunity to save time, to save money, and to have a wider variety of options compared to local stores. These three things convene, or come together, and tempt shoppers to choose these benefits over other strongly held values.

When I consider the health and vitality of my community, however, I recognize the value of supporting local businesses and business owners. I want employees to be paid fairly for the work that they do. It is important to me to shop in ways that help not just myself but other people. I value shopping in a way that creates a community of interdependent people who lean on and support each other.

Convenience is a powerful force. It caters to my impatience. It urges me to think about myself and not my community. If I'm not careful, I find myself enamored by convenience's siren song promising to meet my deepest desires, and I walk away from what's important to me.

Convenience Isn't Everything

When my kids were little and we lived in a rural community, we did a lot of our shopping online. Even though we tried to shop local, our options were limited. One year, we decided to buy most of our Christmas presents online to save time and money. We placed our order more than three weeks in advance, never thinking that our gifts might not arrive on time. That same year, several weeks in a row of terrible winter weather caused shipping delays. Every morning, I would check my email and find the same notice: our shipment of Christmas gifts was delayed due to extreme weather conditions.

The week of Christmas, when our shipment was still delayed, I started to panic. I felt guilty for stressing because it seemed so materialistic, but I also kept worrying about my kids waking up on Christmas morning with nothing under the Christmas tree. We did not have a mailbox at our house. In our rural community, almost everyone had a post office box instead. I received a shipment update three days before Christmas alerting me that the package had been transferred to the United States Postal Service. It was supposed to arrive on Christmas Eve. The problem? Our post office had limited hours the week of Christmas, and there was a solid chance our shipment would arrive at the post office after hours. I imagined the box sitting in the back room of the post office on Christmas Eve, behind locked doors. So close but still out of our reach.

The night of December 23, I got a phone call from the post office. They were closed already, but our package had arrived. The woman on the other end of the phone had a suspicion that the box contained Christmas gifts, and she made a special trip to deliver it to my door. As she handed it to me, she said, "I thought about your kids on Christmas morning, and I thought they would be happy to get whatever is in here." She cared because she knew me.

When I shop online or at a big-box retailer, the merchant views me as a consumer. I am a number, a potential spender of money, but I am not a person with a story. Even when these convenience retailers try to personalize their services, the impersonal nature finds a way of coming through. I recently needed to contact a company about a problem I was having with a product. I visited the company website to find a phone number for customer service but was directed instead to a chat bot. This bot tried to handle the problem digitally by searching for keywords as I typed. After a long, unproductive "chat" session, a human being replaced the bot on the chat interface and helped me with my problem. Even when a person was helping me, the interaction felt impersonal. A rhythm of shopping based on a producer-consumer model will leave us wanting for human connection. As we choose what is quick and convenient, we may find that we are losing interpersonal connection and interdependence as we shop.

The choice to prioritize convenience is a choice to deprioritize the human side of shopping. I put convenience in my online shopping cart, but I add unintended items to my basket too. I choose the ease of the digital shopping cart, but in so doing, I watch as my dollars leave my local community. I don't *intend* to shop in a way that enables unjust retailers to use child labor or pay unjust wages; but the more I purchase certain products, the more these retailers will continue their practices in order to make a sale. In our globalized and hyperconnected world, sometimes we have no choice but to shop in convenient ways. But when we prioritize this rhythm of making transactions, we make building up our local communities more difficult.

Again, I am grateful for the way online shopping helps those who are unable to shop in person for whatever reason. I give thanks for the way technology has provided better accessibility to resources. For some, these online retailers are not providing mere convenience but access to essential items and services. The problem isn't online shopping in itself; the problem is getting caught up in a rhythm of depersonalized and transactional living rather than the sacred pulse of neighbor-oriented living.

When I try to break the convenience habit, I am almost always surprised by the results. I find baristas who learn my name after meeting me once. I get a front-door delivery from a person who wants my kids to have Christmas presents. I meet people who become my friends. And I purchase products that can be fixed locally by people who see me as more than just my pocketbook. Sometimes these in-person shopping experiences are inconvenient. I have to step away from my habits and routines and take a risk. Sometimes I have to pay a little bit more. But I have found it is almost always worth it. Convenience isn't everything.

The Cost of Convenience

When the rhythm of our shopping is a rhythm of convenience, we gravitate toward what is good for ourselves privately. We choose faster delivery, lower prices, and seemingly limitless choices, even when opting for those things has consequences for ourselves and our community. We do this for the efficiency, for the monetary savings, and to have a wider variety.

Convenience shopping saves time—either time spent looking for the item in stores or time spent waiting for the item to arrive. In a world with overfilled schedules and the expectation of twenty-four-hour availability, the convenience of being able to shop when I want from wherever I am is tough to pass up. With online marketplaces offering nearly everything, it is possible to buy everything in one place, which saves on trips to different stores or even time spent searching

on other websites. I can go online to Amazon and within
minutes add books, groceries, yard tools, furniture, and clothing to my cart. I can even buy music, movies, and television
shows. Local businesses cannot keep up with places that
specialize in everything. Some of the big-box stores have
tried to make this one-stop shopping experience available in
brick-and-mortar locations around the country and around
the world, but even they cannot keep up with online retailers
with their global networks and partnerships.

Something like 87 percent of people are influenced by
delivery speed when considering an online purchase. In one
study, a business was projected to see a 0.73 percent sales
increase by offering one day faster shipping. By contrast,
if the company offered one day slower shipping, sales were
projected to drop by 0.51 percent. While these percentages
might seem small, they work up to big numbers. One day
faster shipping had the possibility of bringing in thirty
thousand more orders, which would mean about nine mil-
lion dollars in added revenue. Consumers want faster delivery, and online shopping works to make it happen. There is
no doubt that online shopping can save time—especially
when you factor in driving time, time wrangling children in
and out of the car if you've got kids, the time spent looking
for the item, and the time spent waiting in line to check
out. But many times, online shopping doesn't save as much
time as we think it will. And even when the time-savings is
undeniable, it is good to ask whether the time saved comes
at a price we are willing to pay.

Convenience shopping often saves money. The cold,
hard reality is that I can save a bundle on pretty much any

item if I buy it online. If I go into an independent book-store, I'm going to spend more on the same book than if I buy it from an online retailer—at least, most of the time. If I go into a big-box store with a vast selection of items, I'm going to be able to buy a shirt for a fraction of the cost than if I bought it somewhere else. I'm not much of a shopper, but I have still experienced the thrill of scoring a great deal. But buying something for less money isn't the same as buying something justly.

I'm not much of a seamstress, but I have dabbled in sew-ing. The first clothing item I made for myself was a skirt made out of a simple black and white fabric. I bought a pattern, fabric, a zipper, matching thread, elastic, and additional fabric to line the skirt. I walked my items up to the checkout. The cashier rang up my total, and that's when I had a realiza-tion: it was going to cost me more to buy all these items than if I had gone to Walmart and bought the exact same skirt off the racks. How was it possible for an item to cost less than the cost of materials?

The answer was something I did not particularly want to confront. The only way I could get an item for such a low price was if someone, somewhere, was treated unjustly. The manufacturer found a way to get both the materials and the labor needed to produce the item for a fraction of what either was worth.

Author and professor of Catholic studies at DePaul University William T. Cavanaugh recounts a story about a woman who worked at a factory in El Salvador. The woman made 77 cents per jacket making jackets that sold in the United States for $178 apiece. He writes, "The factory is surrounded by barbed wire and armed guards. A worker interviewed after her 12-hour shift told of being unable to feed herself and her three-year-old daughter adequately. Her daughter drinks coffee because they cannot afford milk; both mother and daughter suffer fainting spells."The president of the company that owned the factory acknowledged the injustice of paying the workers so poorly but excused it as necessary to keep the jackets at a price Americans were willing to pay. We may go through times in our lives when money is tight, and we have to cut costs wherever we can. But when we habitually spend less money on items than what those items are worth, we come to expect our purchases at a price that is either unsustainable or perpetuates injustice. I come to expect a dress for ten dollars when the cost of materials would run me forty dollars. I spend a couple of dollars on food when it was something that had to be grown, tended, and sometimes even harvested by hand.

Prioritizing monetary savings encourages me to keep the dollar signs in my sights rather than the value of items I buy and the people who produced them. As people called to live with persistence, we must push against the constant bombardment of advertisements encouraging us to think only about saving money. We must ask hard questions, dig in, and do research. What does it gain us to score a great deal if we forfeit what matters more? By becoming intentional as we shop, we may spend more on specific items, but we will be paying what they are worth. And in so doing, we are persisting toward justice.

Convenience shopping also promises a vast selection. When a retailer sells everything, buying things becomes a one-stop shopping experience, which saves time and the hassle of making multiple trips. But there are also trade-offs. First, a shop that offers pretty much everything specializes in none of it. When you buy something from one of these megaretailers and it breaks down, finding someone to fix it is a major problem.

My grandpa owned a typewriter and office supply store. As technology rapidly evolved, his store could not keep up with all of the computerized changes. But when you bought a typewriter from him, you could bring it to him to be fixed when something went wrong. You could find replacement pieces and ribbons and correction tape, and if you weren't sure what you needed, a knowledgeable person could help you get the right thing. The specialization of his store and his skills meant he was able to develop a relationship with his customers and help them with their typewriters over the course of their lives—not just over the course of one transaction.

When we choose to shop at megaretailers, we lose out on the connections and relationships of community-based shopping. I remember going to the grocery store with my mom when I was younger. If we ever had a question about a fruit or vegetable, we could ask the produce department person. We talked to the person behind the meat counter as we talked about what was on sale that day. We got to know the people who rang up our groceries. We asked them about their lives, and they asked us about ours. I know this small talk isn't for everyone, but what stands out to me is that the relationships and community of those childhood shopping experiences are nearly absent from the way I shop today. Convenience shopping may be easier, but it is also lonelier. It centers only on what is important to me in that moment, and it neglects the vibrance that is possible when we move and live in community.

Moving away from a rhythm of convenience to an other-centered way of shopping is difficult. In many cases, it is a day-by-day decision, sometimes even hour-by-hour. Convenience is . . . well, convenient. Or as Walter Brueggemann puts it, "Extracting money from the local economy is characteristically 'convenient'!" Making our financial decisions from the long-view perspective of what is good not just for me but also for my community will be inconvenient at times. This may tempt us to give up. But we can choose to be persistent.

A Posture of Persistence

In Luke 18, Jesus tells a parable about a widow who is seeking justice from a judge. The problem? The judge "neither feared God nor had respect for people" (Luke 18:2). This unjust judge stands in the way of what the widow needs, and so she returns to him time and again asking for justice. Eventually, she wears the judge down and he gives her what she seeks, not because it's the right thing to do or because he's had a change of heart, but because he is tired of her bothering him day in and day out.

Parables like this one are a perfect example of why we should not treat parables as allegories. If every person in the story stands for something, who is the unjust judge? Surely not God. But who else would the widow petition every day until she was finally heard? Perhaps knowing we might be confused without an explanation, Luke tells us what the parable is about before we've even had a chance to hear the story. He writes, "Then Jesus told them a parable about their need to pray always and not to lose heart" (Luke 18:1).

The widow gets up every day and pesters the judge who doesn't care about her situation because justice matters to her. She will not rest until she is heard. If we look at this parable from a time-saving perspective, we see that the widow's actions are inefficient and inconvenient. Surely she had better things to do than bother the judge every single day. But Jesus tells us this parable to teach us the importance of persisting in prayer and justice. Perhaps it seems a stretch to talk about this parable when looking at shopping, but sometimes I wonder if we overspiritualize Jesus's teachings. Yes, this parable is an encouragement to keep praying. But what did the widow pray for? Justice.

When the disciples asked Jesus how they ought to pray, he taught them the Lord's Prayer. This prayer was intended not only to teach us how to pray but also to change the way we live. In the prayer, we pray for God's kingdom to come and God's will to be done on earth as it is in heaven. And who has God called to do God's will and bring glimpses of the reign of God here on earth? That would be us. Who is to forgive our debtors? We are. Jesus taught us to pray bold prayers in faith because prayer makes a difference, but he also taught us to pray bold prayers so that we might find the courage to live with the same kind of boldness with which we pray.

The parable of the persistent widow is about the importance of prayer, but it is also about the importance of becoming persistent people. Justo L. González, author and retired professor of historical theology, writes that Jesus does not teach us to persist in prayer so that we will be "'blessed' with a fortune as a result of insistent prayer" but so that we might find the strength to carry on in the face of injustice when "vindication seems illusory." In a world of discouragement, injustice, and inequity, Luke 18 is an encouragement for us to develop a posture of persistence. The word that is sometimes translated as "lose heart" is a compound Greek word that means "becoming discouraged when we don't receive the outcome we hoped for." I imagine the widow in need of justice felt like giving up many days when the judge refused to grant her what she needed. I can almost imagine the walk home after he shut the door in her face, and I can hear her inner dialogue encouraging her to drop the whole thing. Why try? It's hopeless anyway. This is the kind of discouragement Jesus addressed with this parable, the kind of discouragement and disheartenment that makes you want to quit trying altogether.

In the impulsiveness fostered by convenience shopping, we make choices that have a lasting impact. We send our dollars out of the community rather than investing in it. We make it more difficult for local retailers to stay in business and pay their employees. In the moment, it seems beneficial to make these shopping choices. And there may be benefits. But we often don't weigh the consequences first. When we expect to receive whatever we want in a couple of days, our perspective changes from the long view to the immediate. We become short on patience and lacking in persistence. We even become less creative as we buy things rather than make do with what we have.

Prior to seminary, my husband and I lived in the Chicago suburbs, where you could find pretty much anything you wanted. There were specialty markets and stores of all types. There were restaurants of every variety—including a restaurant where customers hoped to be insulted by the table servers. Grocery store aisles were filled to the brim, and there was never a time when I couldn't find all the ingredients I needed for a recipe.

After three years of seminary, we moved to a small town. The first time I went grocery shopping, I felt shocked. I couldn't find everything on my shopping list! Eventually, after living in that community for eight years, we developed a new rhythm—one that was patient and had different expectations. And I can honestly say that rhythm was life-giving. We learned to make things at home. We made decisions to go without if we couldn't find what we were looking for. We ordered some things online, but not every retailer would deliver to our address. It turned out that I didn't need to have the world at my fingertips in order to be happy. The first time I went back to a grocery store in the city, the number of choices almost sent me into a panic. Once I had learned to go without, having all of those options available to me didn't feel like a gift. It made me anxious.

The rhythm of shopping for convenience is a rhythm that is ultimately about *me*. It is about my convenience, my time-saving, my money-saving, my endless options. We may not always have a way around convenience shopping, but I think that should give us a little bit of pause. As we tap into the sacred pulse of community-oriented shopping and transactions, we will move away from a lifestyle of *me* toward a habit of *we*. What builds up my community? How can I meet my needs while doing so justly? Is it possible for me to form a network of people who are working toward this same goal so that we might share with each other, help one another, and offer encouragement along the way? Finding ways out of the fast track of convenience and back to the intentional pace of community is tough. But it's also sustainable. It encourages creativity and relationships. It urges us to ask what is truly important to us: quick and convenient, or long-lasting and just?

Being able to purchase anything we need at the click of a button is a blessing. Sometimes we need to be able to shop that way. It might be a sanity-saver, something necessary because of our situation, or a temporary help during a tough time. There is no shame in that. But finding a rhythm of justice, patience, and creativity as we step away from the allure of unlimited convenience will nourish our spirits and our relationships in ways we didn't even know we needed. Perhaps what we need is not a coming together of all our conveniences but a coming together of people, convictions, and imaginations as we seek to bring the kingdom on earth as it is in heaven.

5

COMPOSITION OF MAKING

The Holy Rhythm of Handcrafting

I walked to my great-grandma's house after school when I was in middle school. She lived right across the street from the school, and as I walked the short distance to her house, I could see her through the picture window in her front room, sitting in her rocking chair. Granny's house was a place where time seemed to stand still. As her chair rocked rhythmically to and fro, the pendulum of her cuckoo clock would swing back and forth with a rhythm that seemed to match.

She effortlessly moved a crochet hook along the project she was working on—quite often a blanket with a chevron pattern. Granny had poor eyesight, but she could feel each stitch as she made her blanket patterns from memory. I would sit in a chair near my Granny while she crocheted.

We would talk about my day at school, and we would watch whatever was on her small television set in her living room. I was in awe of the way she could take strands of yarn and make them into a masterpiece, all while being mostly unable to see. Most of the time, she wasn't even looking at her stitching anyway. Each stitch she made was natural; it flowed from her mind and her heart into her hands, and somehow the hook did the work of creation.

After a while, I grew curious about how crocheting worked. Granny made it look so easy that I wanted to try it for myself. Granny got out a scrap ball of yarn and an extra hook (anyone who crochets or knits knows you can never have too many hooks or needles), and she taught me how to crochet a chain. Because she could not see the stitches well, she could not teach me how to start the second row. I caught on to making chains, and soon I was making crochet chains along with my great-grandma every time I came over after school. I would show off my endlessly long chains with pride—hundreds of stitches I had strung together—when my mom came to pick me up. Even though I have no use for those chains today, I wish I had kept at least one. As I crocheted with Granny, her whole house seemed filled with rhythm and motion—the rocking chair, the ticking clock, and our bobbing hooks moving in and out with the work of making. Somehow, with all of that rhythm and motion, time seemed to stretch out, each moment filled with more space and breath than the one before it.

Years later, as a college student, I had a roommate who taught me how to knit and later to crochet. I was never very good at knitting, and it took a lot of effort for me to learn how to crochet well enough to make anything useful. But something about picking up a hook and yarn again made me feel connected to Granny, who had passed away years before. Something about feeling the yarn slide between my fingers while I stitched it into something new put back together parts of myself I didn't know had come undone.

Wholeness in a Fraying World

So much has changed since those afternoons at my great-grandma's house. No longer do moments seem to stretch and hold more than what seems possible. Instead, my moments seem to be overflowing with more tasks and expectations than they can contain. If I turn on the television or spend much time online, I find myself overwhelmed by the chaos and the never-ending avalanche of difficult events in the news. At times, I find myself grasping at all the frayed ends in the world and trying with everything I am to hold them all together. In the midst of being overwhelmed, I look inward to search for something immovable, unbreakable, and constant.

What I find is that just as the wind from God hovered over the formless void before the dawn of the new creation, so too does the Spirit hover over the chaos and struggle in my life, just waiting to make all things new. Just as I did at Granny's house so many years before, I pick up a crochet hook and a ball of yarn. I find a place in my house, and I allow the rhythmic motion of the crochet hook, and the gentle movement of my fingers, to stitch something together where there had been only formlessness before. When everything seems to be falling apart, creating with my hands helps me put something new together.

In the very beginning, God chose to make human beings in God's image. This puzzling phrase—"the image of God"—has led to much wondering and to the writing of many books. At its most basic, it means that God created us to share something in common with God, albeit in a fragmented and imperfect way. Thomas Merton wrote about the image of God in this way: "To say that I am made in the image of God is to say that love is the reason for my existence, for God is love. Love is my true identity. Selflessness is my true self. Love is my true character. Love is my name." When we read about God in the pages of Scripture, we are learning not only about who God is but also about who God made each of us to be. In the poetic telling of creation in Genesis 1, we learn that God is both Creator and creative. In the rhythm of the movement from night to day, the placing of the stars and the sun, the forming of the animals, and the creation of human beings, we learn that God is an imaginative God. When we involve ourselves in the work of making things, we are connecting to the imaginative and creative image of God stamped on each one of us. By using our creativity, we are living more fully into the image of God, the image that leads us to become more fully who we are.

The work of creativity is the work of restoration. When we are creative—whether in an artistic endeavor or in the way we approach problem-solving—we are living more fully into who we are as people created in God's image.

When we involve ourselves in the work of creativity, we draw closer to wholeness, closer to who God created us to be. Or as writer Madeleine L'Engle said so well, "The discipline of creation, be it to paint, compose, write, is an effort towards wholeness." In a literal sense, when we make things, we put things together. We stitch yarn into a blanket that keeps us warm. We paint a picture that brightens our living space. We put together a grocery list that helps us feed our bodies. We come up with inventive ways of getting tasks accomplished so that our lives have more freedom and joy. But in another sense, our inner division and scatteredness begin to heal as we explore the creativity within us. We learn more about who we are. We discover the stretchiness of time. We trade the idea of human beings as producers for the balm of human beings as makers. We are not merely doers; we are dreamers.

At some point in our lives, we will all meet at least one person who has moved toward wholeness. We will know it when we meet them, even if we cannot articulate it. We will experience the stretching out of time when we are with them. We will breathe more deeply as we are seen and known by them. We will be inspired toward creativity, compelled toward imagination. I have been privileged to meet a few such people. One who springs immediately to my mind is someone who has feasted on the words of the poets and the imagery of Scripture. Her mind is always percolating with a question or a wonderment. She writes words on scraps of paper as insights occur to her. Her bookshelves are filled with her book friends who have helped her to find the way. She doesn't think herself special for the things she does, but you cannot help but be inspired by the way the world inspires her. I am renewed when I spend time with her because she reminds me of what it means to be human, to be one created in God's image, to be one who was made to wonder and imagine.

Theologian and writer Frederick Buechner believed that when we encounter people who have discovered "another way of being human in this world, which is the way of wholeness," we would understand at once what we were seeing. He wrote, "When we glimpse that wholeness in others, we recognize it immediately for what it is, and the reason we recognize it, I believe, is that no matter how much the world shatters us to pieces, we carry inside us a vision of wholeness that we sense is our true home and that beckons to us. It is part of what the book of Genesis means by saying that we are made in the image of God."

It seems paradoxical to say that we find the end of our journey by looking back at the beginning, but I believe it is true. As people created in the image of the Creator God, we discover anew who we are by embracing our calling to be creative people. We embrace a fuller picture of ourselves when we remember we were created to imagine and to make.

Speaking through Creativity

After watching a movie in a darkened middle school classroom, our teacher turned on the overhead lights as he said, "Let there be light." The whole class laughed. Our teacher had merely flipped the light switch back on, but his words reminded me of the way God brought light into the world: by speaking. Imagine with me the formlessness before the first day of creation. The primordial deep churned as God's breath swept across the surface of the waters. The chaos was interrupted by the voice of God, which called things into order. First the darkness and the light were separated. Next the sky was created as the waters were separated above and below the dome. Each time God created, God spoke order and beauty into existence.

When we make things, we do not speak them into existence in the same way, though I do believe our words have the power to shape the world. Instead, we take our cue more from Genesis 2. In it, the Lord God "formed man from the dust of the ground, and breathed into his nostrils the breath of life" (Genesis 2:7). God commissioned the first humans to till and keep the earth, to get their hands dirty. Human beings were made to work with their hands.

Even though our words do not breathe new worlds into existence, the connection between speaking and creation remains intact. When we are creative, we allow our innermost selves to speak. In our creativity, we give voice to whispers buried deep within ourselves; we learn more about who we are. I first began writing when I was in elementary school. I had finished reading *A Wrinkle in Time* by Madeleine L'Engle, which awakened within me the realization that words can create entire worlds into which we can escape. I first tried my hand at science fiction. I wrote some strange stories about a land with red aliens and white aliens, separated by a river. After a while,

I tried my hand at poetry because it seemed to bend the rules of reality much like science fiction did. I found that no matter what genre I tried, I discovered things I didn't know I already knew.

Anyone who has written much of anything will tell you that stories take on a life of their own, and this is true. The writer begins with an idea in mind, but the story never develops the way the author imagined (unless the author refuses to let the story lead, and these are the dullest stories). I think this happens because stories exist within us and beyond us. But I also think this happens because we know these stories inside of ourselves, even before we are aware that we know them. When we write, we allow these stories out. We meet them and discover them, and we realize they had been part of us all along.

When we create—whether we think we are artistic or not—we allow the voice we keep hidden to speak, to bring ideas together, and to make something new in this world. For the writer, these things may come to life in the form of stories, poems, and books. For an artist, our inmost selves might speak by creating paintings and drawings. For the yarn artist, we might speak by putting together blankets and hats. For someone who cooks, we might arrange ingredients and recipes to make food that nourishes us well through the week.

I have taken to making prayer shawls for people I know who have either been diagnosed with cancer or who are caring for someone with cancer. I don't make them terribly often. It's not a discipline per se. But every now and then, when I learn that someone is facing a challenging diagnosis and all my words fail me, I sit down to make a prayer shawl. As I stitch, there is something about the rhythm that helps me quiet my mind. All of the swirling thoughts and emotions are directed into prayers and love for the person who will receive the shawl I crochet. In those chaotic and heartrending moments, crocheting helps me give voice to emotions inside of myself that I haven't yet figured out how to speak. My words do not do any creating, but my creating helps me find the words. As Stephen King once wrote, "I write to find out what I think." This has been true for me, both with writing and other creative pursuits. We often do not know what we think, or how we feel, until we express it by making something.

Author Steven Pressfield recognized the power of the discipline of creativity. He writes, "When we sit down day after day and keep grinding, something mysterious starts to happen. A process is set into motion by which, inevitably and infallibly, heaven comes to our aid." We pull up a chair at our desk, pick up some yarn, or reach for a paint-brush, and at times it feels like we are doing nothing more than grinding away at whatever it is in front of us. Yet it is in the discipline of showing up to the creative table that the miracle happens. Sometimes that looks like a story spring-ing forth and making its way onto the page. Other times, the miracle is that we begin to understand ourselves better. We give voice to our innermost selves in ways we had been unable to do before. We more fully embody the image of God, whose creativity inspires our own. By making space in our days and in our lives for working with our hands and imagining new possibilities, we are making space within ourselves for our most complex thoughts and emotions to speak. As we put together whatever it is we are making, we are also putting together pieces of ourselves in ways that resonate and reverberate with song.

As a clarinetist, I struggled to practice my music on my own. I would sit in the enclosed practice room in the conservatory of music with its blank, institutional walls, and I would struggle to play. I discovered later that my struggle was not with the notes themselves but with being unable to hear the song. I needed to hear it all put together. Once I listened to the piece, I could better play my own part. Then as I practiced, I could put together in my mind the whole composition.

When we create with our hands, the compartmentalized, separated parts of ourselves come together so that we can hear the whole song. We spend our days separating the work parts of our lives from the home parts and the serious parts of ourselves from the playful. When we make something, we allow all of our pieces to come and create at the artist's table. As we do, we discover that our whole selves inform our creative work, even the parts of ourselves we had forgotten about. Musician and storyteller Andrew Peterson says, "Those of us who write, who sing, who paint, must remember that to a child a song may glow like a nightlight in a scary bedroom. It may be the only thing holding back the monsters." And I think he's right. But I also think our songs, our words, and our art may glow like a night-light that shows us what's truly there in the dark and not only what our imaginations fear. Making something new lights up the path we are walking on, and it illuminates parts of ourselves we often fear. In the making of our art, in the honing of our craft, we turn on the lights and see ourselves as we truly are.

Rough Drafts and Masterpieces

Every one of us is an artist, though many of us have forgotten the imaginative parts of ourselves. "All children are artists," Madeleine L'Engle writes, "and it is an indictment of our culture that so many of them lose their creativity, their unfettered imaginations, as they grow older." When we first begin to create, we have not yet learned to compare ourselves to others; we have not yet learned to belittle what we make.

When my daughter first learned to write her name, she made her lowercase a's look like flowers. They weren't "correct," but they were beautiful, and they were hers. Eventually, she learned to conform to her teacher's expectations, but a part of me was sad that her name no longer contained those flourishes. As a child, I wrote songs to the hum of the vacuum cleaner while my mother cleaned. I was about four years old, and I didn't care whether my lines rhymed or my voice was off-key. Somewhere in between age four and age ten, when I sang my first solo at church, I had learned to be afraid of the song within me. I was so nervous before I sang on that Sunday morning that my stomach filled with knots. We are born with an inclination to be creative and quickly learn to get in our own way. We learn to be afraid of what others might think, and we learn to doubt the ability that each of us has—whether we write, sing, crochet, or make things in other ways.

What often gets in the way is perfectionism. We may sit at the keyboard or stare at a blank screen for hours and not know in that moment what holds us back. In Anne Lamott's brilliant book on writing, *Bird by Bird*, she calls this internal roadblock out for what it is: "Perfectionism is the voice of the oppressor, the enemy of the people. It will keep you cramped and insane your whole life, and it is the main obstacle. . . . I think perfectionism is based on the obsessive belief that if you run carefully enough, hitting each stepping-stone just right, you won't have to die. The truth is that you will die anyway and that a lot of people who aren't even looking at their feet are going to do a whole lot better than you, and have a lot more fun while they're doing it."

I fear opening myself up to the creative process because I am afraid of failing, or not measuring up to the expectations I have for myself—or the expectations I think others have for me. So rather than try, I struggle to allow myself to begin.

In Ephesians 2, we read that we are "God's handiwork, created in Christ Jesus to do good works, which God prepared in advance for us to do" (Ephesians 2:10 NIV). We are God's *handiwork*. The word that is translated as "handiwork" is the Greek word *poiema*, which is where we get the word *poem*. One translation renders this word "masterpiece" to capture the intention of *poiema* (NLT). As beautiful creations of God, we were created to do beautiful things. And yet sometimes that idea feels more like pressure than a gift. Most days, I feel less like a masterpiece and more like a rough first draft. We may compare ourselves to others who have accomplished something amazing earlier in their lives than we did. Or we might think about our mistakes, or our imperfections, and fear that we will never measure up.

The trouble is that we read verse ten of that passage without reading what comes right before it: "For it is by grace you have been saved, through faith—and this is not from yourselves, it is the gift of God—not by works, so that no one can boast. For we are God's handiwork" (Ephesians 2:8–10 NIV). We are not God's masterpieces because we've written books, or made hats for every kid in the elementary school, or kept perfect scrapbooks of all of our experiences. We are God's masterpieces because of God's grace. And because of God's grace, we can dream and imagine and create with courage. We—who are merely dust—are beautifully created, wonderfully made, and wholly loved. Even as we struggle to be creative, or wonder if it is worth putting the pen on the page, or doubt that our pictures open up worlds for anyone besides ourselves, we are beloved people called to set free the creativity we have been given. We have forgotten what God can do with dust. Rumi's words reflect my own when he writes, "You think you belong to this world of dust and matter. Out of this dust, you have created a personal image and have forgotten about the essence of your true origin."

Too often we want to pretty up the rough draft before we've even put the words on the page. We want to show the world a masterpiece before we've allowed our dust to be on display. Ultimately, though, we've gotten it backward.

We have convinced ourselves we have to create a master-piece before we will be accepted. We have forgotten that we are masterpieces because of grace, and not because of anything we have done.

When I was a first-year student in college, my first class during my first semester was a class on writing. I had always loved writing, which made the thought of having to be all the way across campus and ready to learn by 8:00 a.m. less intimidating. A few weeks into the semester, I got my first paper back with the lowest grade I had ever received in my life. The comment at the top of the page said, "Needs revising." I was frustrated. I had never revised anything before! I turned in another paper (without revising it), and my teacher asked me to stay after class. He told me, "April, you could be a great writer. You just need to learn to slow down and revise." I stiffened up (probably to avoid tears), and I left the class burning with anger.

For several years, I didn't realize why I reacted to his words the way I did. As a fledgling college student, I thought the way you overcame the fear of making some-thing new was by convincing yourself what you were making was already beautiful. I thought the key to the creative life was to believe what you made was already a masterpiece. No dust included. I have since discovered that the true courage an artist must find is the courage to cover the page with dust with the faith that somewhere within the dust is a treasure to excavate. God created me a masterpiece even if my creative work still needs refining.

Until we find the courage to receive grace and let our imperfections hang out, we will either create nothing at all or we will create thin shells of what could be—all the while believing them to be fuller than they are. We are already God's handiwork now, in this moment, whether we've written enough books to fill a shelf or we're still staring at a blank page. We are already God's beloved creation, even if we skip a stitch and have to unravel three whole rows to fix it. We are already God's artwork, even if we don't think we have a creative bone in our bodies. And when we mess up, there's grace—and a red pen so we can get to revising.

The world we live in can be a hostile place for creativity. We may wonder if, in the face of all of the chaos and heaviness around us, our small works of imagination and making are worth doing. We may doubt we have anything to offer. I struggle with these doubts too. But I also remember those afternoons at my Granny's house where time stretched on and the pulse of life was comforting. I remember my middle school struggles falling away at her door and the pride of holding up my ridiculously long crochet chains, which were completely impractical but beautiful and beloved all the same.

6

BREATH MARK OF SNOW DAYS
The Holy Rhythm of Free Time

Many days in western Nebraska are beautiful, and the sun shines more often than it doesn't. The sky is blue and expansive, and the landscape is breathtaking. Don't let anyone try to convince you Nebraska is flat and boring; anyone who says that hasn't been off the interstate.

But for all Nebraska's spectacular attributes, the weather can be extreme, unpredictable, and volatile. A gust of wind blowing ninety-four miles per hour once folded our backyard trampoline in half. Hailstones the size of golf balls (even baseballs on occasion) have leveled entire cornfields. The rain seems to be either scarce or torrential. A couple of years ago, the end of May saw a day with a high of eighty degrees followed by a snowstorm that snapped limbs and downed power lines just days later. It is not unusual for the temperature to fluctuate thirty to forty degrees over the course of twenty-four hours. Nebraskan people are tough and have a can-do spirit; not much slows them down or gets in their way. They have had to learn to roll with whatever punches the weather gives them.

Out here in Nebraska where you can experience all four seasons in one week's time, we pride ourselves in very rarely taking a snow day. We know how to get creative and find ways to get the job done even when the weather seems bent on working against it. But even here, when the clouds roll in and the snow closes the roads, sometimes the only thing you can do is hunker down and stay home.

As a kid, I loved snow days. I welcomed them as a reprieve from the daily grind. They meant more time at home, more chances to do things we could only do on the weekends—like reading a book in one sitting or having a LEGO battle with my brother. As an adult, snow days have become more complicated. Even when the weather closes things down, there is still work to be done. Things got trickier as an internet connection became a staple in many households and as smartphones made their way into nearly every pocket. Even when travel is impossible, much work can still be done remotely. When circumstances prevent in-person meetings, technology makes meetings possible via email, phone conference, or video chat. My childhood memories of snow days as the cosmic eraser that wiped the calendar clean were quickly replaced by my adulthood experience that some expectations don't go away when bad weather strikes. Those tasks simply shift to new platforms.

But what if it doesn't have to be this way? What if snow days are not an obstacle to overcome but a gift to be received? How might we receive the blessing of a calendar wiped clean, a deep breath of unexpected time?

In a piece of music, sometimes you will find little marks that look like apostrophes scattered across the page. These marks are breath marks. Their purpose is to help instrumentalists and singers identify the places where they can breathe, or lift, or pause just for a moment. These marks help the musician play the musical lines as the seamless phrases the composer intended. Breath marks are designed to show you where to breathe. In a relentless piece of music with few rests written in, musicians need the reminder to take a breath. Breath marks give that permission. Once you have practiced a piece of music often enough, the breath marks become so ingrained that when you get to those places, you won't be able to do anything other than fill your lungs and breathe. I am reminded of Lao Tzu's thoughts on the empty spaces: "Clay is shaped to make a pot, and what's useful is its emptiness."

Snow days are like breath marks scattered throughout the otherwise hectic and frantic pace of life, letting us know it is OK (and necessary!) to breathe. In an ideal world, we would not need to fight against snow days or find a way to get our work done in the midst of them. We could receive snow days as gifts that help us reset, start anew, and clear off an evening or even a whole day to spend in ways that give us life.

Snow days are often inconvenient. Sometimes they derail plans that are important to us. At times, they cause us to miss out on opportunities. Sometimes snow days are a huge pain that require us to make up work down the road. And sometimes snow days come with a real cost—lost wages, canceled plans, lost opportunities. But even in the midst of these challenges, snow days provide us with a moment to breathe, an opportunity to create space. For a control freak like me, snow days offer a chance to experience the freedom of letting go.

What if, as we received the gift of an unexpected snow day, we allowed ourselves to be reoriented toward what matters most in our lives? Perhaps by receiving the gift of unexpected free time, we will allow ourselves to let go of hindrances we hadn't even realized were holding us back.

Freedom of Letting Go

I often respond to an unexpected snow day (or another situation that wipes my calendar clean) with stress or anxiety rather than childhood joy and relief. Canceling meetings means rescheduling meetings or finding new ways to hold them. Inclement weather often means pushing the gift of free time to the side and moving business online. Instead of handling these work-related tasks from the office, I end up handling them from home, with all of the attendant stressors and distractions. My expectations, or the expectations others have for me, collide with reality, and when that happens, disappointments, stresses, and fears come out—often in unhealthy ways. Brené Brown captures the essence of this: "But in those moments when disappointment is washing over us and we're desperately trying to get our heads and hearts around what is or is not going to be, the death of our expectations can be painful beyond measure." Rather than allowing expectations to die, I cling more tightly to them—to my own detriment.

Many of us begin our days with all kinds of unspoken expectations. We may plan to make progress on a project at work or to take care of something around the house. We might make a goal of choosing healthier snacks or of planning our meals more wisely. We may begin our days with expectations others have placed on us—deadlines, responsibilities, and obligations. When something happens that makes it difficult or impossible to make meeting these goals a reality, we experience loss or a sensation of being out of control. Letting go of unspoken plans and aspirations is painful. For me, as a pain-avoidant person, I would sooner take my meetings and conversations into a digital format while the dog is barking in the background and the dinner is burning than allow those meetings to be rescheduled or canceled. I would sooner punish myself by putting too many irons in the fire than allow my plans to drop or be changed.

Why?

I used to believe that my desire to get it all done no matter the obstacles was the product of my work ethic. I grew up watching how hard the people in my family worked, and I learned how to work hard too. I believed that when difficulties were thrown in your path, you were supposed to respond by working harder. Later, as I noticed my difficulty to embrace rest and take time off, I thought perhaps the culprit was my personality. Even though I am a creative person and enjoy little bits of spontaneity, I am also a major type A perfectionist, and I thought this explained everything. I thought the voice inside that said "keep working even though the circumstances have changed" was my inner perfectionist. I thought my aversion to snow days and cleared calendars was just the way I was wired. Maybe *some* people could enjoy the break from the daily grind, but those people weren't me. It turns out, however, the problem goes a lot deeper than that.

My resistance to receiving the breath of an unexpected snow day is because I struggle to believe I am beloved just as I am. Because of this, when I would take the free time I was given, I would experience feelings of shame or guilt because I didn't think I deserved the gift. By working hard, I hoped to prove myself loveable and worthwhile. I held out hope that whatever deficits I might have might be made up for by doing something that counts. I don't think I would have said it that way—certainly not out loud—while I was busying myself sick. But once I found myself unable to keep up the pace, I realized my work ethic wasn't really a work ethic, and my personality wasn't responsible either. I pushed through the obstacles as a way to cover all the things I wanted to hide from others—and from myself. It was the way I chose to cope with my nagging sense of inadequacy.

Two little verses from Ephesians 5 had helped me justify my "ethic" of working myself sick: "Be careful then how you live, not as unwise people but as wise, making the most of the time, because the days are evil" (Ephesians 5:15–16). These two verses yanked out of their context served as a nice justification for not taking time away from my work. Wisdom meant making the most of the time, which I decided meant being productive. And why was it important to live this way? "Because the days are evil." I convinced myself that "making the most of the time" meant making every minute count for something productive. Not only is this mentality unsustainable, it is not even in keeping with the intention of these two verses.

The word translated as "making the most" is a word associated with the marketplace. The word means "to buy something up," "to save it from being lost," or "to redeem something." The same word is used in Galatians 3 to describe how "Christ redeemed us from the curse of the law by becoming a curse for us" (Galatians 3:13). So what are we supposed to redeem or save from being lost? Time. But not just regular old time: *kairos* time—the opportune moments. The fleeting moments that are here and then gone. It turns out that productivity is not the only way to redeem opportune and fleeting moments before they slip away. Sometimes we redeem the time by recognizing the sacred moments for play, for creativity, for a nap on the couch, or for having a snowball fight.

Once we are able to let go of our expectations, snow days and other unexpected calendar-erasers may become gifts of God's grace. For a brief moment—maybe even a whole day—we are invited to step away from the daily rhythm of work and experience something different. When we are able to let go of our expectations and embrace the deep breath of free time, we are set free from our bondage to our calendars and plans. Even though calendars and plans can be gifts too, they can easily become the bandages we use to conceal our self-doubt. As we loosen our attachment to our expectations, we open ourselves up to receiving the gift of free time, the gift of unexpected space for out-of-the-ordinary things. Someone once told me that the key to having no resentments was expecting nothing from anyone. While it may never be possible to expect nothing from anyone, I think he was right that our expectations can quickly become resentments. When we let go of our tight grip on our schedules, we will find the freedom to receive each moment as it comes.

The Peace of Perspective

When snow days come along, we have to let go of our expectations and our desire for control. Snow days offer us the gift of perspective, but we are often unable to receive this gift because we are gripping too tightly to the reins of our lives. Most of the time, we go through life believing we are solidly in control. We convince ourselves that we have everything figured out. But when unexpected challenges come along that are beyond our control, the illusions of our all-figured-out lives come crashing down.

Perhaps you're chuckling as you read this. Snow days hardly seem like something to lose your cool over. But maybe it isn't snow days that remind you of how little you control. It might be the storm that causes the electricity to go off or the flat tire that strands you at home for the day. Or maybe your child gets sick or a family member needs help and you have to take an inconvenient day off. No matter what it is that comes along and clears the calendar, each of us will experience times in which our plans have to change. Each of us will bump up against the desire for control that lurks within us. Snow days come along and cancel plans we've made, and our reaction is often to push harder for whatever it is we wanted in the first place.

Control can easily become an idol. We cling to it because it makes us feel safe. As an idol, it needs to be toppled and torn down because it gets in the way of what's real and important. Imagine control as some kind of towering sculpture on a high platform. It looms large. When you stand at the base of it, it seems majestic and strong. But when you find the courage to topple it, suddenly you can see everything quite clearly. With the idol of control pushed away from view, we gain the gift of perspective. We move away from a life led by our own impulses toward a life guided by something beyond ourselves. As Henri Nouwen writes in a book on spirituality and prayer, "Dear God, I so much want to be in control. I want to be the master of my own destiny. Still, I know that you are saying: 'Let me take you by the hand and lead you. Accept my love and trust that where I will bring you, the deepest desires of your heart will be fulfilled.' Lord, open my hands to receive your gift of love. Amen."

Until we push through the pain of toppling the idol of control to the ground, we will miss the perspective God has for us. We will lose sight of God's love and leading, and we will miss out on savoring the moments—the *kairos* moments—when the daily schedule is pushed out of the way. We will miss those glimpses of God's grace that come to us in ways we would never have expected.

During one particular winter while I was living in Iowa, our weather got into a rhythm of dumping snow on our area every Sunday night for about six weeks. The weather would be great in the morning, but by evening snow would blanket the town and the highway. Every Monday and Tuesday for six weeks, the wind blew so ferociously that it caused whiteout conditions. Every Monday and Tuesday for six weeks, school had to be canceled. The first snow day was fun. We were excited for the unexpected time at home with our kids. We built a snowman and made hot chocolate. We played board games and watched movies. The second snow day was fun too. By the third week of snow days, we struggled to find the same joy.

I began to understand why the psalmist wrote in Psalm 23:2, "He *makes me* lie down in green pastures" (emphasis mine). Sometimes the only way I will lie down and receive the breath mark of a snow day is when God makes me. That year, God made us lie down in green pastures—or inside our house—a lot. Week after week. We were tired of having our schedules forcibly rearranged, our routines tossed out, and our days unpredictable and chaotic. We were longing for the routine of normalcy. In the absence of it, I tried to forge ahead and get things done. I tried to force my normal life into these abnormal situations, and all I did was make myself frustrated. I am sure I frustrated my family too.

The reason I pushed so hard to keep things routine and ordinary was because I was afraid of letting my idolatry—my worship of control—fall to the ground. I was afraid of what my life would look like if I loosened my grip. What I found, however, was that the tighter I held on to my way of doing things, the unhappier I became. I grew angrier, more resentful, and short-tempered with the people around me. When my plans seemed to be unraveling, I responded by trying to hold all of the fraying ends together. For a short time, it worked, but it wasn't until I found the courage to let go of my desire to be in control that I could receive the gift that was being offered to me. When the idol of control fell off its pedestal, I could see more clearly. I laughed more, I said yes to an extra game of Skip-Bo "golf," and I let the kids stay up late while we watched a movie. Unexpected time allowed us to make some of our favorite memories.

The Joy of Space

Snow days are a breath mark in the midst of our busy and frantic lives. They give us permission to breathe, refocus, regroup, and spend our time in life-giving ways. If our circumstances allow us to stay home, why do we panic with the news that the roads are closed, the flight is canceled, or the buses aren't running? Sometimes it's our expectations clashing with reality or our tight grip on the idol of control. But sometimes our panic is because we choose to focus on what we have lost rather than on what we have. We dwell on the grief of expectations unmet and routines disrupted. Acknowledging our disappointments and our griefs is important, but when we linger there—especially in the case of momentary inconveniences—we lose out on joy.

In *The Life-Changing Magic of Tidying Up*, Marie Kondo writes about making a shift in her life as she sought to simplify and tidy her home. When she began her decluttering journey, she focused on getting rid of things. She looked at everything around her as a potential source of clutter. She set about ridding herself of clutter wherever she found it. Yet her home still felt untidy, and she was miserable. It wasn't until she stopped thinking about getting rid of things and started becoming intentional about which things she *kept* that she began to find joy in her life. She writes this: "I had been so focused on what to discard, on attacking the unwanted obstacles around me, that I had forgotten to cherish the things that I loved, the things I wanted to keep." When we are presented with something that changes the course of our day, we can choose to focus on the loss. We can focus on that canceled coffee date, the postponed meeting, or the interrupted moment. We can choose to be consumed by regret, longing, and envy—even if all we are envying is our own made-up life, and not someone else's.

Or we can choose something else. We can choose to breathe. As we breathe in our expectations, we can exhale and let them melt away. Instead of choosing to think about what we no longer have, we can look around and see what *is* there. What is right in front of us? What opportunities for beautiful moments exist right here and now, things we would have missed out on if life kept moving the way we had expected? We can pause and allow our lives to be filled with the space that brings us joy. Sometimes it takes the removal of all the excess for us to be able to treasure what we've always had. Our inclination is to forge ahead, to push through the pauses, to keep on going even when we desperately need to stop and catch our breath. When our calendars unexpectedly clear, the breath mark invites us to breathe deeply and receive the joy that is only possible when we make space for it.

Simone Weil, French mystic and activist, once reflected that "grace fills empty spaces but it can only enter where there is a void to receive it, and it is grace itself which makes this void." The trouble is, I am an expert at packing the empty spaces in my life so full that there's hardly room for grace to get in. Anne Lamott describes grace "as a ribbon of mountain air that gets in through the cracks." But I was used to filling those cracks, not realizing that I was keeping myself from receiving grace at the same time. Too often I approach my schedule like a game of Tetris, where all of the pieces must perfectly interlock with no empty spaces leftover. Sometimes it takes a snow day, or some unexpected holy interruption, to make space for us to receive the grace that will bring us joy. Sometimes it takes an unexpected snow day to Marie-Kondo all the busyness so we can breathe deeply the joy of unexpected time. When all the plans overflowing our schedules are removed, we are offered free time as an opportunity to breathe and to receive the joy of moments pregnant with possibility.

For a few years, I had wanted to get some backyard chickens. I researched my town's zoning laws and learned all the ins and outs of raising chickens for fresh eggs. The one thing that kept me from taking the plunge was a lack of time. Everyone told me that baby chicks take a lot of effort, at least for the first couple of weeks. You have to make sure the brooder temperature is just so or the chicks will be either too hot or too cold. In the first few days of life, baby chicks can get themselves into trouble, and you have to be ready to intervene. Once the chicks have grown enough to be kept in a coop and run in the yard, they need fresh water and food every day. By then they do not require as much daily effort—at least as long as all of them stay healthy. Every spring I would think about getting baby chicks, and then I would talk myself out of it because I just didn't think I had time.

When everything began shutting down at the beginning of the COVID-19 pandemic, I spent the first few weeks trying to regain my bearings as all our routines disappeared. Some meetings and activities moved onto online platforms, but other things simply went away. Evening meetings were cleared from the calendar. Kids' extracurricular activities were on hold indefinitely. Suddenly the one thing I had a whole lot of was time. It felt like simultaneously too much free time and not enough time all at once.

Somewhat impulsively, I told my husband that I wanted chickens. We no longer had the excuse of not having enough time. We didn't have a coop yet, and we had no idea how to make one. But we decided to go for it. So we went to the store and bought four Easter Egger chickens and supplies for a chicken brooder.

Now, many months later, even though many meetings have started to refill my schedule and my busier routines are taking shape, I have made an evening ritual of hanging out with my chickens in the backyard. I open up the chicken run and watch as they stretch their wings, race around looking for bugs and grass, and fluff up their neck feathers at each other as they play fight. I walk around the yard and talk to them. I laugh at them. Occasionally I pick them up and stroke their feathers. And then, as the sun starts to lower in the sky, the chickens go one by one back into their coop to roost for the evening.

I had held off doing something that would bring me joy because I had stuffed my life too full. And when all of those things fell away, I realized how much more full life was—full of peace, perspective, and joy—when I ended my nights watching the chickens play in my yard. Even before they had laid any eggs for us, they brought me more joy than I ever could have imagined. I only wish it hadn't taken a global pandemic for me to make space for something that mattered to me.

In a society that prizes workaholism and round-the-clock availability, it is countercultural to breathe deeply and savor the breath marks life gives us. We might avoid pausing and breathing because we are concerned it will cost us something. And it might. We may not move up the ladder. We might not be able to participate in every opportunity that sounds interesting or important. Or perhaps we do not lean into joy because we feel guilty spending these moments on ourselves. We might feel wasteful or self-indulgent, especially if we can't identify a higher value or an altruistic purpose in what we're doing.

The sacred pulse of snow days, and other moments of unexpected free time, urges us to breathe deeply and find joy in life because joy is worth pursuing. When we do this, we will have gained the gifts that only space and free time

can provide: the perspective and joy of a life rooted in
the present moment. Because this is where life is—in this
moment, in this day, in this hour. We are often just too busy
to keep our eyes and our hearts in this moment where we
find ourselves. As we practice breathing with life's unexpected breath marks, perhaps we will develop the habit of
breathing deeply even when we are not presented with an
event that clears our calendars. We may even find ourselves
clearing off an evening or an hour just so we can breathe in
deeply and experience the joy of unfilled space.

PART III

THE DANCE OF
BELONGING

7

MOVEMENT OF COMMUNITY
The Holy Rhythm of Interdependence

In the beginning, there was connection. God created the world and entered into relationship with it. More deeply, when God created human beings, God did so personally, forming the dust of the ground into the first human being. After the creation of the first person, God saw that humanity was not intended for solitude. Rather, "it is not good that the man should be alone" (Genesis 2:18). God created woman to be man's *ezer kenegdo*: a helper with a strength corresponding to man's own. And Adam rejoiced because "this at last is bone of my bones and flesh of my flesh" (Genesis 2:23).

Later, these first human beings spent time with God. They heard God walking in the garden. They talked with

God. They listened to God. They were in relationship with God. And even when these first humans transgressed the boundary set in place for them, God went in search of them. When their nakedness made them feel ashamed, God clothed them. From the very first breath breathed into the nostrils of the very first person created, human beings were made to be part of a community. We were made for belonging and for relationship. We were made to depend on God and on each other.

Kaitlin Curtice, in her book *Native*, wisely recognizes this truth: "When you are born, you come into the world connected to somebody." Even though we cannot look back and remember that initial physical connection, I believe its memory is stamped on our hearts. "No matter who we are or where we come from, we are people who journey," Curtice writes. "We long for community; we long for oneness with the sacred. We long to be seen and known and to see and know the world around us." From the moment we each take our first breath, we are dependent upon someone else. We rely on someone to nurture us, to meet our needs, and to show us what it means to be human—what it means to be interdependent. Some of us may not have had positive experiences with our earliest relationships. Some of us still carry deep wounds and unmet needs. Others may have learned early what it looked like to love others and be loved in return. No matter our earliest experiences, each one of us was created with a need to belong to something bigger than ourselves.

Despite our need for community, many of us may struggle to find a place where we belong. We may find ourselves holding onto skewed ideas about what it means to give and receive. Or we might find it a struggle to remain connected to people who are profoundly different from ourselves. Circumstances might lead us to endure seasons of profound loneliness and isolation. Even when we experience moments of community, we might struggle against the current of Western society, which is largely individualistic. Wherever we might find ourselves—whether it is a time of deep connection and belonging or a time of profound longing to be known and loved—all of us experience moments when we are pulled away from the sacred pulse of community.

Isolation and Echo Chambers

When I was a sophomore in high school, my family moved to Utah. My brother and I started at our new schools, and my family began looking for a church to attend. We tried a few churches, and I remember my mom asking people after each worship service what kept them coming back week after week. After an uplifting service at one of the churches, my mom approached someone seated near us and posed her usual question. The woman's response? "We are all of the same mind here. No one ever disagrees about anything!"

We never went back to that church again.

When people get involved with each other, there are only two ways to avoid disagreements: for people who disagree with the majority to keep their opinions to themselves, or for the group to be closed off to anyone who thinks differently. We decided that even though we didn't want to seek out conflict and disagreement, a community that never had any was missing out on something—whether that be an honest sharing of perspectives or a diversity of people who see the world through different eyes. It was important to us to belong to a community with a variety of opinions and thoughts rather than an echo chamber where everyone was expected to think alike.

One of the barriers we face when it comes to moving with the sacred pulse of community is the temptation to surround ourselves with people exactly like ourselves. Social psychologist and public theologian Christena Cleveland puts it this way: "These days, Christians can easily go their entire lives without spending time with those who are different from them. Unfortunately, the more we spend time with people who are essentially identical to us, the more we become convinced that our way of relating to both Jesus and the world is the correct way." When we only see things one way, and when we surround ourselves with people who also see things the same way, we miss out on seeing a fuller picture.

Sadly, we might not even know we are missing anything. Our inclination to isolate ourselves from differing points of view meets up with the ease of curating our social media feeds, and soon we find ourselves in echo chambers where all we hear is the sound of our own voice bouncing back at us. We unfollow, block, and defriend our way to a solitary point of view, but in doing so we become myopic. In our desire for peace and harmony, we instinctively block out any voice that might challenge us, ruffle us, or push us to see things in a way that might get under our skin. Sometimes it is necessary, for our mental health, to distance ourselves from painful or harmful conversations or perspectives. This is true especially for those who are marginalized. Community isn't about embracing things that wound us. Sometimes we avoid interactions out of necessity, but many times we are quick to block and slow to listen.

Moving toward community means developing a willingness to get a broader, fuller picture of the world. Are we reading authors who challenge our perspective? Are we listening to people whose experiences do not confirm our own? Have we developed the courage to keep listening, even when we don't like what we hear? Or are we safely nestled in our echo chambers that we have mistaken for communities?

In 1 Corinthians 12, Paul likens the fledgling church to a body. He writes, "For just as the body is one and has many members, and all the members of the body, though many, are one body, so it is with Christ" (1 Corinthians 12:12). And yet it is to this same early community that Paul wrote strong words of correction and instruction because its members were mired in conflict, disagreement, division, and struggles for power. While Paul urges them to be united in Christ, he does not tell them to put their differences aside. Instead, he uses the imagery of the human body to encourage the church to see the value in each one of its members. He writes, "As it is, there are many members, yet one body. The eye cannot say to the hand, 'I have no need of you,' nor again the head to the feet, 'I have no need of you'" (1 Corinthians 12:20–21). We need every single part of our body—of our communities—and we cannot flourish unless the whole body is flourishing, for "if one member suffers, all suffer together with it" (1 Corinthians 12:26). Being part of a diverse and multifaceted body will involve conflict and pain, but that doesn't mean we should neglect or ignore the parts that are suffering. Instead, we must listen to our bodies—to our communities—so that we can find healing and strength together.

In our increasingly polarized world, we face the temptation to ostracize anyone who disagrees with us on anything. We *do* need to weed out ideologies and relationships that are harmful or toxic. But many times we confuse disagreement with toxicity. When we shun all disagreement, we shut out dialogue, communication, and a diversity of perspectives. The result of rejecting differing viewpoints is a hollowed-out community that is more like staring at our own reflection in a mirror than working together as part of a varied and beautiful body.

An oft-quoted and widely attributed saying urges, "In essentials unity; in nonessentials liberty; in all things charity." When it comes to essentials, unity is important. The trouble is, we do not always agree on what things are essential. And even when we can find a common understanding of what the essentials are, we often have a hard time allowing others liberty when it comes to the nonessentials. And how charity is in short supply!

If Twitter is to be believed, all my viewpoints are essentials, and anyone who disagrees with any of it is to be canceled, ostracized, or questioned about the validity of their faith. Agreement itself, rather than the substance of our views, becomes essential. Groups built around conformity and total agreement are affinity groups rather than bodies. The primary goal of these groups is to reinforce already held beliefs rather than encouraging questions, doubt, and growth. By contrast, communities that are vibrant and healthy bodies will include varied members and perspectives, not to the group's detriment, but to its strength.

The sacred pulse of community draws us out of our echo chambers and into relationship with other parts of the body. When we build community, we will not merely tolerate differences of opinion; we will seek them out because we understand the limited and finite nature of our own perspectives. As we do this, we may find resistance within ourselves. Broadening our horizons is difficult. People might view the world in ways that anger us and send our defenses up. But we need each other. We need to see the world through each other's eyes. We need to close our mouths more often than we open them. We need to listen more than we speak. We must find the courage to replace our social media platforms with tables where we can share with people who are different from us, even if those differences challenge us in profound ways. As we set our tables for community, we do not need to make space for harmful perspectives or hateful ideologies. Yet we must be careful not to throw out all disagreement or difference in perspective in the process. Growth happens when we allow ourselves to be stretched and challenged. In the absence of growth, we become stagnant waters—breeding grounds for shortsightedness.

Giving and Receiving

It may be "more blessed to give than to receive," but often it is more difficult to receive (Acts 20:35). When we give, we experience the satisfaction of helping someone else. When we give, we experience a sense of euphoria or happiness—triggered by the release of chemicals in our bodies such as oxytocin—that can last for weeks at a time. Even pausing to remember the act of giving can trigger these feelings all over again. Giving lowers stress hormones in the body, which leads to better overall health and a boost in immune system function. The act of giving rewards us physically and psychologically, which makes us more likely to want to give again.

Researcher Allan Luks called giving-related happiness the "helper's high" in the 1980s, and that phrase has stuck. Giving not only helps others; it helps us too. Even though giving comes at a cost—we have to give something up, whether it is time, money, energy, or something tangible—that cost does not go unrewarded.

Receiving, on the other hand, is a risk. When we receive something—whether it is something large like an unexpected monetary gift or something small like a compliment—we have to open ourselves up to receive it. We have to allow ourselves to be vulnerable. Even though psychiatrist M. Scott Peck first wrote these words in the context of escalating military tensions, they speak directly to the difficulty we often have with allowing ourselves to receive from others: "Our strategy needs to be far more complex and multidimensional than 'peace through strength.' Specifically, we need to pursue additionally, with at least equal vigor, the 'peace through weakness' strategies that build community. Otherwise there is no hope. For the reality is that there can be no vulnerability without risk; and there can be no community without vulnerability; and there can be no peace—ultimately no life—without community."

Giving to others is much like striving for peace through strength. We take the initiative. We are in control. Giving is on our terms. But if we are not also willing to be vulnerable—if we are not also willing to receive from others—we lose out on the reciprocal nature of community. When we are unwilling to receive, we are unwilling to let our walls fall down. We are afraid to be vulnerable.

When I first went to college, I got a crash course in vulnerability. After too many sleepless nights and too much stress, I developed a case of bronchitis that lasted almost an entire semester. Right when I'd think I was healing, I would relapse and become so sick that I could hardly get out of bed. I was so fatigued that I struggled to wake up early enough for my morning classes. I would miss breakfast in the dining hall and stagger into class looking like I had just rolled out of bed (which I had). After a week or more of this, one of my friends started snagging a bagel on her way out of the dining hall. Our cafeteria allowed you to take one piece of food with you after each meal, and she would use that option to make sure I got breakfast. She'd cover a napkin with encouraging notes and pictures, and then she'd wrap up the bagel like a care package inside the napkin. We didn't have the same morning classes, but she would put the bagel on my desk so I would see it when I woke up. Sometimes she made sure she ran into me on the way to my first class. I'm pretty sure I only ate breakfast that semester because she made sure to feed me. Determined to make my own way in college, I found it hard to admit I couldn't do it all. Every morning as I ate breakfast on the way to class, I was both humbled and thankful that I had someone looking out for me. I needed it.

I was used to being a giver. I helped people when they needed something. I shared my lunch with friends at school when they forgot theirs. I lent a listening ear when someone I knew was going through a hard time. I went on work trips to other countries to help people. Suddenly, when I needed help, I realized how hard it was for me to receive. Up until that point, I thought I was helping because I had a good heart, and I still want to think that I had the right motivation. But I realized that helping is easier than being helped. I helped because I could, and it gave me a sense of pride and power.

To move in step with the sacred pulse of community, we have to be willing to receive, not just give. If we cannot receive, our giving is merely charity and not relationship. Brené Brown, a leading voice on the topic of vulnerability, writes, "Until we can receive with an open heart, we're never really giving with an open heart. When we attach judgment to receiving help, we knowingly or unknowingly attach judgment to giving help." We may not realize we are attaching judgment to receiving help until we find ourselves in need of help ourselves. True community requires both a willingness to give and a willingness to receive. Giving feels safer; receiving means the walls have to come down.

Created for Interdependence

As children grow into adulthood, we want them to be independent. I feel myself bursting with pride as my kids learn to do things by themselves. They have learned to tie their own shoes, brush their teeth without help, read to themselves, and—more recently—email their teachers when they have questions about their homework. I have celebrated each of these accomplishments as they take steps on the way to independence. Independence is worth celebrating.

Yet many of us internalize the idea that asking for help is a sign of weakness. I have struggled not to view leaning on other people as an admission that I am deficient. After all, we are supposed to pull ourselves up by our own bootstraps, right? In our individualized society, we have created many clusters of isolated people trying to do almost everything on their own, and we have called it independence. We encourage ourselves and others to develop our own routines and habits, as though none of us exists as part of a wider community. We say, "you do you!" We know that "no man is an island entire of itself," but we largely live our lives as though we were. We talk about "finding ourselves." We focus on personal career paths and getting ahead. When we meet someone, we introduce ourselves by what our occupations are or our educational background and professional credentials. We hone our online personas and perfect our "personal brand." This exclusive focus on our individual lives can make it difficult for us to reach out and allow other people into our lives.

When we moved to Nebraska, seven different neighbors stopped by within the first few weeks to introduce themselves. They brought homemade bread and cookies. Someone brought me a flyer for a community event they thought my kids would enjoy. We exchanged phone numbers and got to know each other. I felt welcomed and loved.

But recently, I had a conversation that changed my perspective. As we were talking about cultural diversity and our different upbringings, one of the people said that in her home country of Japan, neighbors do not welcome you to the neighborhood when you move in. Instead, it is customary for you as the newcomer to take initiative to bring gifts and introduce yourself to your neighbors. While this difference in custom is a cultural difference, it also helped me to understand my own self-focus when I moved to Nebraska. I made the move about me. It was about my new home and my experiences. By contrast, the custom of the newcomer greeting the neighborhood recognizes that the community you've moved into is already in motion. Neighbors have already established reciprocal relationships with one another. When the newcomer reaches out first, it communicates to the neighborhood a desire to become an active part of the community.

The dominant Western church has internalized a narrative of individualism. Some denominations emphasize a personal relationship with Jesus. Others focus on finding each individual person's spiritual gifts as a way of personal discovery. We define ourselves by our individual accomplishments and talents rather than by who we are as part of a wider community. A hyperfocus on individualism causes us to miss out on the broader picture of what it means to be who we are in relationship with each other. We are made to be part of a community. We are created for interdependence.

Rather than individualism or codependency, we are invited to strive for interdependence, a balance of personal well-being and communal belonging. Interdependence encourages and celebrates independence and personal growth but also recognizes that we are stronger together than we are alone. Together we are a body. Together we can move and act in the world in ways we can't do on our own. When we get caught up in individualism, we end up living fragmented, isolated lives. As Chuck DeGroat, professor of counseling and Christian spirituality at Western Theological Seminary, puts it, "So the challenge today is to find wholeness right where we are—in the world, amid broken and divided souls like us, and in imperfect churches with imperfect pastors and imperfect singing and imperfect community. . . . And while we may separate from others for a time, we must recognize that wholeness never comes in isolation." The sacred pulse of community moves us toward interdependence as we learn to discover who we are, both as individuals and within the context of the communities where we find ourselves.

As we saw in chapter 3, Vivek Murthy, former surgeon general of the United States, began noticing a trend of social disconnection and loneliness among the people he talked to, many of whom were suffering ill health in part due to their profound loneliness. This led Murthy to study loneliness in more depth, and he classified loneliness as a health epidemic due to its prevalence. As part of his research, he uncovered a connection between loneliness and violence, and this connection has unsettled me ever since I first discovered it. Murthy cited a study in which researchers "planted the idea in subjects' minds that they'd be alone in later life or that their fellow subjects had rejected them." The result was that people began to ostracize those they believed had rejected them. They separated themselves from the other subjects by "lashing out" at them or "by deriding those they believed had rejected them." While more extreme violence—such as violent crime—is a very rare response to loneliness, a connection has been made in some cases of violence to social disconnection and lack of belonging. We are made for community and belonging, and in the absence of it, we may react with hostility, anger, or even aggression. When we belong to something that is bigger than ourselves, we find meaning and purpose in ways that we simply cannot do on our own.

Despite the prevalence of social media platforms, we face abundant obstacles to meaningful social connection. We divide sharply around politics. We polarize ourselves according to our religious beliefs. Social media saturates us with conflict and disagreement, and we can find ourselves muting and blocking out all of the voices that disagree with our own in order to quiet the noise. We are more available to each other than ever before, with cell phones in our pockets and computers on our desks, but our hyperconnection has not made us more of a community.

If anything, it has contributed to the fragmentation of our communities as we overfocus on the way we present ourselves online rather than how we relate to each other in real time and in person.

When COVID-19 first began causing surges of infection on the coasts of the United States, most of my meetings—both personal and professional—moved to online platforms. At first, I celebrated this move because it gave me a sense of power and control in an otherwise out-of-control situation. The coronavirus could derail a lot of things, but it couldn't cancel all my meetings! But as the weeks and months progressed, I found myself dreading these virtual gatherings. After only an hour-long virtual meeting, I'd feel weary and sad. Seeing someone's face on a screen and hearing their voice through a speaker simply could not replace being together in person. Being able to see people without being physically present did not feel like a gift; it felt like a reminder of what I was missing. While I remain thankful that technology enables us to connect with each other during a pandemic, I am also increasingly mindful of the ways technology works to convince us we are having our needs for connection met when we are actually more isolated than ever.

As we listen for the sacred pulse of community in our daily lives, we must remember that having *more* points of connection does not always mean a greater sense of community. Connecting to the sacred pulse of community looks like being willing to be vulnerable with one another, to receive as well as give. The movement of community is a movement of diverse voices and perspectives, a resistance against the curated echo chambers that endlessly feed back to us the things we most want to hear. The pulse of community is a beat of interdependence, a mutual sharing and belonging, a healthy balance of independence and reliance on others. In the beginning, when God created all that we see and all that we can't see, God created us for connection. We were meant for belonging. We were meant for community.

8

HARMONY OF FRIENDSHIP
The Holy Rhythm of Relationships

The book of Ruth is about the power of friendship. In the story, Naomi flees Bethlehem with her husband and two sons because of a severe famine. After settling in Moab, Naomi's husband, Elimelech, dies. The situation leaves Naomi and her sons in a bind. With no husband for Naomi, her security and livelihood depend on her sons, neither of whom is married. Now, it is hardly ideal for Naomi's sons to find wives in Moab. In Numbers 25, the women of Moab enticed the people of Israel to worship Baal, and after that time, the Israelites viewed the Moabites (especially Moabite women) as trouble. Naomi's sons marry Moabite women anyway, and about ten years later, both sons (whose names ironically mean "frail" and "sickly") die.

Stuck in Moab with no one to provide for them, Naomi and her two daughters-in-law have two choices: rely on the kindness of strangers or lean on family to help them through their difficult time. Naomi decides to return home to Bethlehem, but this decision is far from a safe one. The journey back to Bethlehem will be treacherous for a single woman, and there is no guarantee she will be taken care of when she returns.

Naomi has begun to travel back to Bethlehem, her two daughters-in-law, Ruth and Orpah, by her side, when she decides to send the Moabite women away. In Moab, these two young women might find new husbands and build new lives. Orpah obeys the urging of Naomi and returns home, but Ruth insists on going to Bethlehem with her mother-in-law. In a verse that is often quoted at weddings, Ruth pledges her loyalty to Naomi: "Do not press me to leave you or to turn back from following you! Where you go, I will go; Where you lodge, I will lodge; your people shall be my people, and your God my God" (Ruth 1:16). Legally, Ruth is no longer obligated to Naomi, but the original Hebrew wording tells us that Ruth clings to her mother-in-law using a powerful word of loyalty—*dabaq*—the same word used in Genesis to describe a man leaving his father and mother and cleaving to his wife. In this profound and seemingly senseless move of devotion, Ruth shakes off expectation, reason, and tradition to form a new family and a friendship with Naomi that will be stronger than any adversity they will face. I imagine every step of the journey back to Bethlehem is filled with mourning for Naomi. And yet as the two women form an inseparable bond of friendship, they find, in Mary Oliver's words, their "place in the family of things."

Friendship is a way of orienting ourselves in this world. Similar to community, friendship is a declaration that human beings were not meant to go through life isolated. In friendship, we choose to share our lives with someone else, not for reasons of obligation or social expectation, but because we have decided life is better with each other in it. That said, even though friendship is something most people would agree is a positive, many people struggle to find friendships in their daily lives.

Loneliness is a growing problem, and many people feel isolated from the people around them. Almost every person goes through a season of isolation at some point. We might face loneliness when we move into a new community, when we've begun a new job, or when we've made some other transition in our lives. But for many people, isolation and loneliness are more persistent—something not marked by life transition but rather a way of life. Regardless of where we find ourselves—in a season of loneliness, in a longer time of disconnection, or with blossoming friendships—the sacred pulse of friendship invites us to dig deeper and listen to what's in our hearts. We are invited to make the journey from loneliness to "oneliness," to find friendship with ourselves, and to embrace the mutuality of friendship.

Alone, Not Lonely

At the beginning of the book of Ruth, Naomi and her daughters-in-law experience profound and life-altering loss. Not only have they each lost their spouses during a famine—crisis upon crisis—they have lost all sense of security. In a time when women had very little way to provide for themselves in the absence of a husband, these three women were left in a desperate situation. Orpah returns to her family of origin to seek provision, while Ruth and Naomi make the risky journey back to Bethlehem.

Once they arrive, the women of the town are shocked at the sight of Naomi. They wonder together, "Can this be Naomi?" And Naomi responds, "Don't call me Naomi, but call me Mara, for the Almighty has made me very bitter. I went away full, but the Lord has returned me empty" (Ruth 1:20–21 CEB). Even with her daughter-in-law steadfastly by her side, Naomi feels alone and hollow. Naomi takes a new name for herself, to reflect the sorrow in her heart and to show she was no longer the person who first left Bethlehem years before. The name Naomi (which means "pleasant") no longer fits. Standing in her hometown with Ruth by her side, Naomi is a stranger to her own life. For Naomi, loneliness has been thrust upon her by famine and through loss.

Being alone is not the same as loneliness. Prior to the late sixteenth century, the word *loneliness* was not a regular part of the English language. The more common word was *oneliness*, which meant "aloneness." Far from having negative connotations, "oneliness" was seen as an opportunity to connect with God and to have space to be with yourself.

Jesus sought out solitude. I remember my Sunday School teacher reading this verse from the Bible: "Jesus often withdrew to lonely places and prayed" (Luke 5:16 NIV). As a child, I thought about Jesus being lonely, and I felt sorry for him. Yet when the disciples or the crowds found Jesus, he sometimes reacted with frustration. If I was lonely and someone found me, I would be happy for their company rather than irritated. It wasn't until I was older that I realized the word *lonely* in this verse wasn't a reference to loneliness; it was a reference to solitude. Jesus was seeking out aloneness, or "oneliness." By withdrawing from the busyness, the expectations of others, and the noise of daily life, Jesus was making space for prayer and for relationship with God. The demands of life were ever encroaching, but he continued the practice of seeking solitude. Jesus did not look for loneliness in the negative sense, but he was not afraid of "oneliness."

I used to avoid solitude because of my fears. When I was growing up, I was afraid of the noises in our house. Whenever I was alone, I was startled by all the creaks and thuds of an empty house. But as I grew older, I felt discomfort when I was alone because I had confused being alone with loneliness. In the quiet of the empty house, I became hyperalert both to the noises around me and to the reality that I was by myself. I believed if I was alone, I must be lonely, and I sought ways to cover over the silence.

Tish Harrison Warren shared a study that shows exactly how uncomfortable silence and aloneness can be. In the study, participants were willing to subject themselves to electrical shocks to take their minds off being alone. While

I don't think I ever would have gotten to the point of shocking myself to avoid being alone, I understand the impulse to hide from solitude. I have turned on a television to fill an empty room. I have opened windows so that I could hear the rustling of the leaves on the trees. I have sung at the top of my lungs in an empty church building just to avoid feeling alone. In our noise-saturated world, solitude and silence can be unnerving at first. While time in quiet alone does not need to be a negative, it takes some getting used to. In order to learn the value of spending time alone, we need to redefine aloneness. It is not about loneliness but rather about oneliness: about finding wholeness and space when we are by ourselves.

Connecting to the sacred pulse of friendship begins with finding peace in solitude. Theologian Richard Foster defines solitude in this way: "the creation of an open, empty space in our lives by purposefully abstaining from interaction with other human beings, so that, freed from competing loyalties, we can be found by God." Solitude is a purposeful making of space. It isn't about being ostracized, not fitting in, or being excluded. It is about finding space when we are with ourselves to find interaction with God.

The sixteenth-century nun Teresa of Ávila viewed solitude in much the same way. She wrote, "Settle yourself in solitude and you will come upon Him in yourself." Sometimes our time spent alone is lonely time, especially if we are alone often. But other times, our discomfort from being alone arises from something different. Sometimes we are uncomfortable with silence because we are used to the noisiness of our daily lives. Other times we are uncomfortable because we are avoiding parts of ourselves. Solitude and oneliness are things we have to work toward, and oneliness is not something that happens overnight. We may need to start small—an hour here or a moment there—as we seek to learn more about ourselves and to make space for connecting with God.

Blaise Pascal is quoted as having said that "all of humanity's problems stem from man's inability to sit quietly in a room alone." While that might be an oversimplification, the point remains. My first year of seminary, I took a weeklong retreat with my seminary class. We went to a convent and spent the week studying the spiritual disciplines laid out in Richard Foster's book *Celebration of Discipline*. As we traveled toward the convent, I started to feel feverish. By the time we arrived, I had completely lost my voice. I may be an introvert, but I am also very social. I struggled to stay quiet, even though I didn't have much speaking voice. After a couple of days, I started to feel better, and the spiritual discipline we were supposed to learn about on that particular day was silence. How perfect. We were assigned the task of finding a place in the convent to sit in solitude and silence for three hours. I had been mostly silent for the previous few days thanks to my case of laryngitis. I didn't think the assignment would be difficult. After all, I had been practicing all week.

I found a spot near an icon of Jesus and sat down. I took out a notebook and a pen. I may not have been allowed to speak, but there was nothing preventing me from writing. As I sat in front of the icon, my pen froze. I couldn't write. All I could do was sit. At first, I felt uncomfortable. I fidgeted where I sat. I adjusted my legs and my feet under-neath my body. And then the tears started to flow. I felt broken and isolated. I felt small and vulnerable.

But soon a sense of peace and love washed over me. Even though I can no longer remember what the icon looked like or what it was that first led to the tears flow-ing, I will never forget the experience of being embraced by the love of God as I sat on the cold, stone floor of that convent all by myself. I had to sit long enough to become so uncomfortable I could hardly take it. After pushing through the discomfort, I was confronted by my insecurities. In my vulnerability, I was wrapped up in the love of God. Even now as I think back on that experience, it takes my breath away. In our noisy world, we may struggle to believe that being alone is different from being lonely. But sometimes that solitude is exactly what we need.

Befriending Ourselves

Years ago, I sat in a chair in my counselor's office and told her about a situation I was struggling to make sense of. She sat and listened quietly. Occasionally she asked a question for clarification or to help me think more deeply about what I was processing. She wasn't the type to give advice, so in the rare moments when she shared an insight, I listened. She said, "April, I want you to think about this situation again; only this time, it didn't happen to you. It happened to a friend. What advice would you give your friend?" I was confused by what she was asking, so she got more direct:

"You are quick to show love and grace to everyone. It's time you show love and grace to yourself."

Befriending ourselves is the first opportunity we have to be a good friend. This is not easy, especially when we are gripped by loneliness. But without befriending ourselves, it will be difficult for us to receive love and friendship from anyone else. Vivek Murthy writes, "The fog of loneliness also blurs our internal mirrors. It obscures our inner strengths, as well as the value that we have to offer, the meaning of our own lives, and the sources of joy and wonder that would normally make us feel connected to the universe around us. This blindness can allow us to drift off course, forgetting what we love about our lives and neglecting to accept and befriend ourselves with the compassion and understanding we deserve." As we grow and change, we discover who we are. That process can be delightful, as we find gifts and talents that surprise even ourselves. Other times it is a painful journey, as we let others down and as we disappoint ourselves. We discover our flaws right along with our strengths.

We face the temptation to compartmentalize our rough spots and imperfections so that others will see only our strengths. The cruel whispers of shame aim to convince us that we would not be loved if others saw all of who we are, and so we hide away the undesirable parts of ourselves. Yet those struggles, those parts of ourselves we conceal, are also who we are. When we respond to parts of ourselves with shame, we begin to believe (whether we are aware of it or not) that we are shameful people. We internalize the story that we are not worthy of love. We no longer listen to the voice of God singing over us that we are good—and not only good but *very good*. In hiding the parts of ourselves that make us feel ashamed, we become estranged from ourselves.

Befriending ourselves means uncovering the hidden places and being honest about what we find there. Honesty does not mean viewing these parts of ourselves through the eyes of our worst critic but instead looks like seeing these things for what they really are—parts of our story. These discoveries might be painful at first, but uncovering what we've kept hidden is the first step in reconciling with ourselves. After taking stock of what we've compartmentalized or hidden, befriending ourselves looks like offering ourselves grace and compassion.

Self-compassion looks at our flaws and our brokenness through the eyes of a caring friend. Self-compassion is not about denying the wrong we've done, and it does not mean that any hurts we've caused will magically disappear; but it will enable us to receive our whole selves, as one unified whole, as who we are. Chuck DeGroat writes, "The elusive wholeness we long for comes as we extend grace and love and compassion to every stranger within us." Indeed, we will find things about ourselves that we had kept so hidden that they were unknown even to ourselves! And when we find those things, self-compassion urges us to receive them with grace and love and kindness rather than shame and judgment. DeGroat continues, "It's true that our wholeness is cultivated in quiet and mindful times, but it's also cultivated in the frantic and frazzling moments—racing to pick up the kids from school on time, cleaning up the dog's mess, waiting out a flight delay. Wholeness is experienced as we attend to ourselves with care in every circumstance." We do not have to wait to show ourselves kindness until we've cleaned up our act. It's in the messy stuff of life that we need our own compassion the most.

Finding friendship with ourselves is like learning the melody of a beautiful song. We rehearse it, listen to it, and sing it again and again until the melody becomes so familiar we can sing it in our sleep. The more we seek out friendship with ourselves, the more we will grow to love our own song. Søren Kierkegaard once said that the "lowest [despair] of all" is when we wish to be "another than [ourselves]." We instinctively cover over or hide our imperfections to protect ourselves from getting hurt. But in hiding ourselves, we also keep ourselves from giving and receiving love. Friendship with ourselves unearths what we keep hidden, brings it into the light, and declares we are lovable anyway—as whole people, not just the images and selfies we share with the rest of the world. Befriending ourselves gives us the courage to sing the song that's ours. Until we learn the melody, we will not be ready to embrace the joy of harmony with others.

The Harmony of Friendship

Naomi and Ruth arrive in Bethlehem with no means and few options. Yet the author of the book of Ruth doesn't want the reader to lose hope. Naomi had left Bethlehem because of a famine, but she and Ruth arrive in Bethlehem at the beginning of the barley harvest, a sign that what once was empty will soon be filled. Even though these two women are not bound by blood or legal obligation, both of them go above and beyond to help each other. They form a friend-ship of giving and receiving; ultimately, their loyalty and steadfastness to one another enables them both to thrive.

Naomi connects Ruth with a distant relative of hers, and Ruth harvests in the fields so that both women will be provided for. Naomi, who has taken for herself the name "bitterness," gives of herself to her daughter-in-law. And Ruth, a Moabite woman who would have been viewed with suspicion as an outsider, shows love and loyalty that goes far above and beyond anything anyone could have imagined. Though the story ends with Ruth and Boaz marrying and having a child, the heart of the story is the friendship of two women who defy the odds and give to one another more than either thought they had to give.

Friendship is about mutual giving and receiving. Of course, as we go through various seasons, there may be times when our friends give us much more than we can give in return. And there may be times when we give more to our friends than we receive back from them. But friendship between people who have each learned to sing their individual songs should ultimately shake out to be melodies in harmony—a mutual giving and receiv-ing. Friendship is not about rubbing shoulders with all the right people or stepping our way up to influence or professional position. It's not about networking and social jockeying. Friendship is about choosing to share of our-selves not because we receive anything material in return but because there is joy in being together. As we give and receive in friendship, we may find that our friends help us and we help them, but this is not the primary goal. True friendship isn't about what we can do for each other; it is about who we are when we are together.

Mutuality can be a struggle. Vivek Murthy notes this when he writes, "Unfortunately, many people confuse friendship with transactional relationships, viewing friends as sources of professional status or material favors." We confuse friendships and transactional relationships, in part, because we are lonely. He continues, "Loneliness, too, can impede mutuality, because when we're lonely, the urgency of our own social need can make it difficult to honor and respond to the concerns of others—even if they are our friends." In other words, because we have not learned to love our whole selves—even the broken parts and flawed pieces—we look to other people to fill those voids and meet needs we may not even realize we have. When we do this, we aren't singing our own songs in harmony with someone else; we are asking them to fill in the gaps in our melody. That is asking too much of the other person and shortchanges ourselves as well. In friendship, we choose each other, not because we need the other person to make us whole, but because together we work toward wholeness.

In the upper room with his disciples, Jesus talked about friendship. He said, "This is my commandment, that you love one another as I have loved you. No one has greater love than this, to lay down one's life for one's friends. You are my friends if you do what I command you. I do not call you servants any longer, because the servant does not know what the master is doing; but I have called you friends, because I have made known to you everything that I have heard from my Father" (John 15:12–15).

Jesus defined friendship with his disciples by whether they did what he commanded them, which can sound like a transactional relationship rather than the kind of mutual friendship we have been exploring. Yet what did Jesus command them? To lay down their lives for their friends. To Jesus, friendship meant giving of ourselves and being willing to lay everything down for the sake of love. Jesus wasn't asking them for one-sided sacrifice; he demonstrated the extent of his love by doing the very thing he asked his disciples to do. And this is the mystery of the cross: Jesus offered his whole self so that human beings might find friendship with God.

The book of Ruth concludes with the marriage of Ruth and Boaz, the birth of their son Obed, and the genealogy from Boaz through the birth of David. Yet the resolution of the story—in my mind—is not the birth of the child but the proclamation of the whole neighborhood: "A son has been born to Naomi" (Ruth 4:17 CEB). Naomi, the one whose grief caused her to become a stranger to herself, is once again full. She sees her future through hopeful eyes rather than bitter ones. In Ruth, Naomi has found a new family—one not defined by blood, or by obligation, but by the bond of friendship. Their friendship is a give-and-take that ultimately restores both of them. Ruth finds the courage to cling—*dabaq*—to Naomi even when it does not make any logical sense. She could have returned to her own family in Moab and started a new life for herself. But instead, she chooses friendship and risks a perilous journey to a place she has never been without knowing what the future might hold.

When we are in seasons of isolation and loneliness, we might feel the sting of the lack of deep and abiding friendship. We might ache to find someone who knows us—flaws and all—and loves us anyway. In these painful times, we can listen to ourselves and look for things that bring us joy. If we take the time to listen to our pain and the desires of our hearts, we will be befriending ourselves in a way that has the power to transform our loneliness into "oneliness." This oneliness cannot replace friendship with other people, but it will help us find the courage to sing our song. Perhaps, as we begin to share our melody with the world, we will find others who are singing theirs. And somehow, as if by magic, their melodies and ours will join together in harmony.

9

REQUIEM OF GRIEF
The Holy Rhythm of Loss

I remember the first time I lost a beloved member of my extended family. When I heard the news, I stood on the playground with my shoulders heaving and tears running down my cheeks. I experienced the desperate realization that this world was not as it was supposed to be. Things were broken, the kind of broken you can't fix just by saying "I'm sorry." I cried until there weren't any tears left in my body, and then I continued sobbing dry tears and heaving my shoulders with a grief more profound than I had ever experienced before. I can't remember if I was alone because I was the only one left on the playground, or if I was alone because the other kids outside were unsure what to do with me. All I remember was that I *felt* alone.

That first experience instilled in me the loneliness of grief. Subsequent experiences reinforced to me that grief was a feeling I had to keep to myself. The jarring shock of losing a loved one would be disrupted quickly with "At least she's not suffering anymore," or "He lived a good, long life." Even smaller losses were tempered with "Look on the bright side" or some other nudge to find the silver lining. The worst comments were the ones that blamed God for the way things were: "God must have needed another angel," or "Everything happens for a reason." I wondered, does that mean God intended it to be this way? What reason could God possibly have for so much suffering?

Early on, I learned that grief and loss were private experiences. And if you took a chance and opened up about your griefs to someone else, the loneliness would be compounded by the pain of learning your griefs were too tender for others to hear. Deep wounds were met with words urging me to move out of sadness and to more comfortable topics.

In Elisabeth Kübler-Ross's groundbreaking book *On Death and Dying*—the book that gave us the five stages of grief (denial, anger, bargaining, depression, acceptance)— she muses, "When we look back in time and study former cultures and peoples, we are impressed that death has always been distasteful to man and will probably always be." The "distastefulness" of death—or even of loss and grief in general—has pushed grief work below the surface for many people, or has caused people to gloss over the pain of loss in ways that have contributed to unhealthy patterns. While I do not believe death and loss were God's original plan for humanity, I *do* believe God has a better way for us than the way of avoidance. The rhythm of loss is not an individual rhythm but is instead a requiem that grows and swells and changes as we process loss both individually and as a community. The movement of loss is not supposed to be a lonely endeavor but something to navigate with the support of others—loved ones who open their hearts to us and tell us, "Me too."

Confronting Our Vulnerability

"I once sat with my anger long enough until she told me her name was grief": although I haven't been able to discover who originally wrote these wise words, I knew they were true as soon as I read them. From a young age, many of us were told not to cry when something hurt or to keep our pain inside until we were in the privacy of our own homes. Sadness is viewed as weakness, as something to cover or overcome. As a person who fears my own vulnerability, I tend to hide my weaknesses from view. If I hide them, I can pretend they aren't real.

Anger, on the other hand, feels strong. It is loud and in charge. We try to cram our sadness into the junk drawer of all our unsightly emotions. But just like the junk drawer pretty much every house has, when you've crammed too many things into it, something always pushes its way back out. For me—and I suspect for many people—anger is what comes out when I'm afraid to let myself sink into sadness. But anger can be a voracious consumer. Anger can be a healthy and helpful emotion, but anger that is a cover for sadness has a way of chewing us up and making us feel like we're in charge while it's doing it. The only way to get through the anger to healing is by allowing ourselves to do the work of grief.

Brené Brown tells the story of a conference on failure held in Norway where a session was led by keynote speaker Ashley Good. During the session, Good asked the audience to share words they associated with failure. Among the words they listed were things like *sadness*, *heartbreak*, and *fear*. Is it any wonder we do not share these emotions and experiences with others? We fear expressing sadness, heartbreak, and fear to others because we are afraid of looking like a failure. We are afraid that expressing our deepest hurts will make us look weak. Interestingly enough, when Good showed the audience a report detailing fourteen failures of the group Engineers Without Borders (EWB) and asked the audience what they thought of the people who shared their failures in the report, the audience responded with words like *courageous* and *brave*. Perhaps we find the sharing of failures and sufferings to be an act of courage because we know how afraid we are of sharing these things with others. We hide our hurts because we do not want to be perceived as failures, but we laud the courage of those who find their way through the fear and share their brokenness and pain.

As I struggled to process difficult emotions and situations privately, I turned to poetry. I even wrote my poems under pseudonyms. I had no intention of reading my work to anyone, but on the off chance anyone happened to find one of my poems, I didn't want them to know I was the one who had written them. I buried my sadness, built walls around it, and hid it under aliases because I was afraid that sadness was an inappropriate emotion. Instead, when I expressed an emotion, it came out as anger. Anger felt strong. Anger felt safe. Anger was the fortress I built around the buried sadness inside, and it wasn't until many years later that I realized the depth of my sadness. It wasn't until I couldn't bury it any longer and it came bubbling to the surface that I realized my sadness didn't need to be avoided. In looking my sorrows in the face, I realized that healing would only be possible if I was willing to receive and accept all of the parts of myself—even the ones I most feared.

On the day Jesus died, the women who had followed him prepared spices and ointments for his burial. After their preparation, they observed the Sabbath, as was their custom. On the morning of the resurrection, they went to the tomb with their burial preparations. I imagine their grief was heavy as they walked to the tomb under the lingering shadows of night. When they arrived, they saw the stone had been rolled away. Their grief must have multiplied as they wondered together what this meant. Had someone stolen the body of the Lord? Inside the tomb, they encountered the good news of the resurrection. At that moment, the women remembered Jesus's teaching—that he would die and then rise again—and they rushed back to tell the disciples. When their Lord had died, the women's hopes had been crushed. When they received the good news of the resurrection, their hopes were crushed yet again as the disciples thought their words to be nothing more than "an idle tale" (Luke 24:11). The first resurrection Sunday was a day where profound grief and overwhelming joy stood hand in hand.

On the heels of this empty-tomb experience, two of the disciples headed toward the town of Emmaus. Along the way, the resurrected Jesus met them, though the two disciples did not recognize him. They talked as they walked the road together, and Jesus explained everything that had happened in recent days. Even though he spent time with them and reminded them of the Scriptures, it was not until he broke bread in their presence that their eyes were opened to see Jesus for who he was. In the breaking of the bread, they recognized Jesus. They saw through their grief and discovered the joy of new life. In the breaking of the bread, the disciples whose hearts were breaking saw Jesus.

Accepting Our Whole Selves

At the beginning of the COVID-19 pandemic, my congregation moved all of our worship services online. At first, this change kept me on my toes and so preoccupied me with figuring out all the technology that I did not take the time to deal with the grief of missing my worshipping community. After months had passed and our services were still being offered only online, the grief overwhelmed me. My husband, Jeff, and I had set up in the sanctuary to record the weekly worship service. We had the bread and the cup on the communion table so we could record the celebration of communion. As I retold the story of Jesus's final meal with his disciples, I held up the bread and broke it. As I placed the broken bread back onto the communion table, I looked at that fragmented and separated loaf, and I felt the brokenness in myself. The grief, the pain, and the struggle of losing my gathered community overwhelmed me. I paused to still my breathing, and then I finished saying the words of institution—the words in 1 Corinthians 11, about how Jesus had broken the bread and shared the cup with his disciples. In the rawness of my grief, I realized that just as Jesus is made known to us in the breaking of the bread, sometimes we are made known to ourselves in the breaking open of the wounds we conceal.

When we are grief-avoidant, we hide and cover parts of ourselves that make us afraid or cause us pain. We bury the parts of ourselves that hurt. We compartmentalize the losses and griefs that would otherwise bring us to our knees. We do this to protect ourselves, but the result is that sometimes we no longer recognize ourselves—our whole selves—because of the measures we take to conceal our pains. We bury our questions, our what-ifs, our losses, and our griefs because we fear them. These broken things are the stuff of our nightmares, and so we close our eyes and imagine more pleasant things. The trouble is, we cannot escape these experiences and these weaknesses. They are inside of us, and they are part of who we are. In covering them, we are hiding from parts of ourselves. This avoidance can come out as festering anger, broken relationships, and numbness.

In John 11, Lazarus becomes ill and dies. This story is often referred to as "the raising of Lazarus," and the focal point of the story is the moment in which Lazarus is raised from the dead. Mention might be made of Jesus weeping along with his friends and the other mourners, but typically we are eager to move on from the grief to the joy of Lazarus being raised to life. Yet the longer I study this story, the more I am inclined to focus on Martha, Lazarus's sister. Remember the story of Mary and Martha in which Mary sits at Jesus's feet and Martha is busy with her work? Growing up, I always heard that Mary was the hero of the story because she was able to rest and be present to Jesus. Martha was portrayed as the anxious sister whose mind fixated on all the wrong things. A closer look at Martha in John 11 dispels this image and reveals instead a woman who could speak about both her grief and her hope in the same breath.

In the story, Jesus learned that his friend Lazarus was ill. Lazarus's sisters sent for Jesus, but Jesus delayed in coming. By the time he arrived, Lazarus had died, his sisters were grieving, and they were angry at Jesus for not showing up in time. Martha heard that Jesus was coming, and she went out to meet him. Martha led with her anger and disappointment when she confronted Jesus: "Lord, if you had been here, my brother wouldn't have died" (John 11:21 CEB). Jesus, where were you? We called for you. We needed you. You weren't there for us. Martha greeted Jesus with these pointed words. Yet she followed them up with one of the most profound statements of faith in the Bible: "Even now I know that whatever you ask God, God will give you" (John 11:22 CEB). I am inspired by Martha's depth of faith in bringing her whole self to Jesus. Martha was present to her anger, to her grief, and to her faith in the midst of an uncertain and trying time. While I may want to sit at the feet of Jesus like Mary, I also want to have faith enough to bring my whole self to God like Martha.

In her little book *Stitches*, Anne Lamott sums it up this way: "Pretending that things are nicely boxed up and put

away robs us of great riches." One of the treasures of peer-
ing into the drawer of our unprocessed griefs is the treasure
of becoming known to ourselves. We may grow up inclined
to avoid our pains, but in acknowledging these wounds as
part of who we are, we become whole people. We become
people with deep wells and hard-won wisdom. Theologian
and writer J. Todd Billings faced a raging torrent of grief as
he was diagnosed with terminal cancer. Billings's children
were very small when he received this devastating diagnosis, and he found both hope and a voice as he looked
to the Psalms. In his book *Rejoicing in Lament*, Billings
shared a reflection he originally posted on the CarePages
website. He wrote this: "This is a place where I find the
Psalms particularly helpful. On the one hand, the Psalms
are honest about our fears, our feelings of injustice. They
don't patch over it with sentimentality. However, they do
not end there. . . . We only fully enter into lament when we
realize that we're not just expressing ourselves to a human
observer but bringing our burdens before the Lord, the
Creator, the Almighty, who—in light of our distress—is
our Deliverer."

When we enter into our griefs rather than hiding them
away, we give our grief legs. Grief that is buried forces its
way back out, and quite often it comes out sideways. Grief
that has legs is grief that becomes part of our journey.
Grief with legs walks alongside us rather than weighing
us down. We begin by acknowledging our pains and our
griefs. These losses are real. Our feelings about them are
real. The heartache and grief are real. Our struggles are not
signs of our weakness but signs that we are human. Facing

these struggles and acknowledging them is a step toward wholeness and away from fragmentation.

After we've brought our weakness and heartache into the light, we may struggle with what to do next. We might wonder how to move forward, especially when the burdens seem too difficult to carry and when the prospect of giving our grief legs seems impossible. When we find ourselves stuck in our grief, the book of Psalms can help us find a way forward. As Billings grappled with his difficult diagnosis, he noticed that the psalmist takes all of the pain, the struggle, and the grief and brings "all of that before the face of God." The psalm writer brings grief, anger, distress, doubts, and despair into God's presence because the psalmist knows God can handle it. We can do the same.

Releasing the Burden

In the Gospel of Matthew, Jesus says, "Come to me, all you that are weary and are carrying heavy burdens, and I will give you rest. Take my yoke upon you, and learn from me; for I am gentle and humble in heart, and you will find rest for your souls. For my yoke is easy, and my burden is light" (Matthew 11:28–30). The word translated as "carrying heavy burdens" is a word meaning "to be weighted down." These burdens are heavy. They weigh us down, and we are weary from straining against them. Jesus invites us to bring our burdens to him, but he doesn't promise that our burdens will disappear. Instead, Jesus offers us his yoke and his burden, which are light. The tough stuff doesn't go away when we come to him. Jesus doesn't tell us everything will get better and all our problems will vanish. When we bring our burdens to Jesus, he offers us his yoke.

A yoke is a piece of wood that joins two oxen together. The yoke helps the oxen share the burden because it distributes the weight between them. In a paradoxical teaching, Jesus calls out to all who are weary from carrying their own burdens and offers to give them a different burden instead—his burden. The twist is that when we are yoked together with Christ, when we bring our whole selves to God—griefs, failures, losses, and all—we will receive a yoke, connecting us to a light burden that will give us rest.

The words of Jesus draw me back to the prophet Jeremiah. God, through Jeremiah, warned the people of the danger to come and urged them to turn back. After verses about impending destruction and loss, this was the word from God: "The Lord proclaims: Stop at the crossroads and look around; ask for the ancient paths. Where is the good way? Then walk in it and find a resting place for yourselves. But you said, 'We won't go!'" (Jeremiah 6:16 CEB).

In the Gospel of Matthew, Jesus invited the people around him—and us—to stop at the crossroads in our lives and look around. What do we find there? Do we find heartache and broken relationships? Do we find pain we are not sure how to deal with? Do we find griefs and losses that cannot be repaired? Where is the good way? The good way is found not in avoidance or in searching for a way around but in taking stock at the crossroads and searching for the good way, the way with the easy yoke and the light burden. When we give our grief legs by acknowledging its presence in our lives and its crushing burden, we can bring it forward with us to Jesus, who promises to take the burden on with us. Jesus's yoke is easy not because all of our difficulties and troubles will disappear when we come to him but because he carries them with us. True rest is found not in the suppressing of our griefs but in making our griefs known to the God who listens, cares, and shoulders the burden with us.

In her insightful TED Talk "We Don't Move on from Grief. We Move Forward with It," Nora McInerny urges us to consider our griefs not as temporary losses but as a part of our life that will always be with us. Our losses and hurts are a part of us, and we can carry these with us while also experiencing joy, excitement, hope, and love. As she talks about the loss of her first husband, Aaron, and the love she has found with her second husband, Matthew, McInerny says this: "All of a sudden, those two plots were unfurling at once, and falling in love with Matthew really helped me realize the enormity of what I lost when Aaron died. And just as importantly, it helped me realize that my love for Aaron and my grief for Aaron, and my love for Matthew, are not opposing forces. They are just strands to the same thread. They're the same stuff." McInerny recognized that our wounds and our joys are all integral to who we are. When we compartmentalize one from the other, we become scattered and distant from ourselves. Healing is found in receiving both parts of ourselves.

Elisabeth Kübler-Ross, decades after writing about the five stages of grief, wrote another book in which she sought to clarify the stages of grief she had written about so many years before. When Kübler-Ross first shared the five stages of grief, many people latched onto them as a sort of "road map" for moving on from grief and loss. The stages were seen as five linear steps, benchmarks one must go through in order to heal and put a loss in the rearview mirror. But grief is not linear, as I said earlier. Our losses become part of who we are, and they change us irrevocably. The five stages of grief were seized upon by people eager to find healing—or to move *others* toward healing—and people began to use them as a way to gauge progress through grief. If someone lingered too long in any of the five stages, or seemed to move backward in their grief process, or if they skipped a stage altogether, they might be urged to get through it more quickly.

Kübler-Ross was concerned by the way her research was being used when she wrote this decades later: "The stages of grief have evolved since their introduction, and they have been very misunderstood over the past three decades. They were never meant to help tuck messy emotions into neat packages. They are responses to loss that many people have, but there is not a typical response to loss, as there is no typical loss. Our grief is as individual as our lives." We may choose to hide our losses away and avoid them, or we may choose to open ourselves up to them, but we will all experience them nonetheless.

There is no road map to navigating grief. We may share experiences and processes in common along our journeys, but no two roads are the same. Whether we have experienced profound grief or are working through a loss of another kind, we face the temptation to avoid or conceal our pains. When we avoid the difficulties, we avoid embracing our whole selves. We hide the painful parts of our stories and become strangers to ourselves. If we do not accept our griefs, we do not accept ourselves. In the Beatitudes, Jesus promised comfort for those who mourn (Matthew 5:4). When we tuck our griefs away, we keep ourselves from the comfort God offers. If you have been on this planet for more than a few years, "those who mourn" likely includes you. I know it includes me.

Learning to uncover and accept our griefs as part of our journey is painful. We may or may not have had healthy examples to follow in those around us. We may be unsure of where to begin. And we may wonder if we have enough courage. While there is no one-size-fits-all way to uncover and accept the parts of ourselves we'd rather hide, I believe we become more known to ourselves when we do. Bengali poet and Nobel Prize winner for literature Rabindranath Tagore once wrote, "Grant me that I may not be a coward, feeling your mercy in my success alone; but let me find the grasp of your hand in my failure." Is it really cowardice? Surely not I, Lord. But perhaps this is why Jesus invites us to take his yoke upon us. The good way is the way in which God's hand grasps hold of ours in the midst of our failures. The good way is the way that leads us to the easy yoke, the light burden, and the tree planted by streams of abundant and living water.

Experiencing God with Us

My first memories of grief were memories of loneliness and isolation. As I reflect back on my earliest childhood experience with grief, I want to whisper to that heartbroken girl on the playground, "You don't need to walk this road alone." The tragedy and the gift of the human condition is that we are surrounded on all sides by those who have felt the sting of loss. Some of us may have become especially skilled at hiding those parts of ourselves away, but those pains are still there. They never leave us. They become part of who we are. And we are not alone in them. I wonder what would happen if we worked to destigmatize sorrow and grief. Would we find our way to express our deepest hurts and fears? Might we have our eyes opened to the pains and hurts of others in ways we never had before? As our eyes and hearts are opened, we may begin to see each other in a whole new way—siblings who are carrying heavy burdens, desperately in need of the rest and respite of God.

We are complicated creatures, fearfully and wonderfully made, carrying both profound joy and immense suffering at the same time. Like Martha, we can bring our whole selves—our pains and our trust—before God. God can handle it. Even though Martha believed all the wrongs in the world would someday be made right, she was not spared from the pain of grief. Our hopes and beliefs do not spare us either. We can hold pain and faith in our open hands, with both of them being true at any given moment in time, because they are both who we are. We can open our hearts to love and joy and excitement while also having our hearts break from loss and grief. Sometimes I find myself unable to believe that I can be beloved in my brokenness. But this is where I can exchange avoidance for the embrace of all of who I am, pains included. This is where the lightness of Christ's yoke eases the pain and lightens the load.

PART IV

THE DANCE OF RENEWAL

10

CRESCENDO OF CELEBRATION
The Holy Rhythm of Appreciation

Emily Dickinson wrote, "God gave a loaf to every bird, but just a crumb to me." This crumb, for her, was not a symbol of what she lacked. She was not writing about how little she had in comparison to others. Quite the opposite, in fact. Dickinson treasured her crumb so much that she could not bring herself to eat it. And she wondered aloud through her poetry whether those who had been given great riches and an abundant feast of bread were able to appreciate the crumbs they, too, had been given, or if the bounty swallowed up the miracle of the small blessings.

In our fast-paced world overflowing with abundance, I wonder if we, too, miss out on the joy of the small blessings. We see the loaves in our neighbors' hands, and we forget to be thankful for our crumbs. I have come to believe that if we do not practice appreciation in the small things in our lives, we will struggle to celebrate the larger things when they come along. But when we dot our days with appreciation, our gratitude will swell into a crescendo of celebration that will infuse our lives with the joy of God.

The creation account in Genesis 1 is punctuated by the repeated refrain "And God saw that it was good." God's work of creation went hand in hand with appreciation and celebration. God the Creator paused to appreciate each part of the creation in much the same way as an artist might pause to celebrate a beautiful combination of colors or an author might breathe a sigh of satisfaction after writing a chapter. We often talk about the way human beings were made to be creative because we are made in the image of the Creator God, but we do not always talk about the way we are also made for celebration and appreciation. God paused to celebrate creation because celebration is important. When we celebrate what we have finished, we are allowing ourselves to rejoice over the good and beautiful things in our lives. Appreciation inspires us to continue the work.

Working on an intensive project requires giving of ourselves. We give of our creativity, our time, our energy, and our discipline. At the conclusion of our work, celebration acknowledges what we have poured out and allows us to be filled back up. When we take time to appreciate a job well done, we are breathing in the uplifting joy of celebration. I am convinced that when we appreciate the small things, and when we celebrate the work we've done, we are also worshipping our creative God who inspired us to do the work in the first place.

Unfortunately, many of us find it easier to criticize the work we've done than to celebrate it. We might sit back and notice all our typos, our mistakes, or think about all the ways we might have done it better if we had it to do all over again. Others of us get stuck procrastinating or putting off the work because a nagging self-critic in our minds tells us we won't do a good job so why even try. Moving in step with the sacred pulse of appreciation leads us away from self-criticism, shame, and perfectionism and toward the life-giving rhythm of celebration. As one who has struggled with perfectionism and allowed it to limit me, I have often wondered why I choose to shame myself and my abilities rather than celebrate the work I've done. I cannot answer this question for every person who struggles in this way, but I wonder if we share something in common. Beneath our self-shaming, procrastination, and perfectionism, I believe there is a smoldering kernel of self-doubt that asks whether we are worth being celebrated.

Neither Perfect nor Shameful

In the beginning, God declared human beings good, but many of us received the message early in our lives that we are not. Whether someone pointed out our flaws, or we internalized a negative self-image because of mistakes we made, many of us struggle to believe that when God created us, God saw that we were good. We focus on our deficits—real or perceived—and we look to external sources of validation. When we begin with a view of ourselves as broken, imperfect, and hopelessly incapable, we will struggle to look at what we do with a sense of accomplishment or appreciation. We will either criticize what we've done and reinforce our negative view of ourselves, or we will be too afraid to do anything at all lest we confirm our worst fears. I've often heard it said that the good news isn't good news unless you first acknowledge the bad news, but I think most of us are already keenly aware of our own deficits and woundedness. What knocks us out of our hopelessness is not the news that we are messed up but the whisper of God's voice over us telling us we are beloved and created in the image of God. What shakes us out of our shame and fear is God's declaration that we are very good, created to thrive and experience joy.

I'm not sure which came first: the feeling that we are hopelessly *not* good, or theology that told us as much. I did not grow up in a church that talked about total depravity—the idea that sin and fallenness affect every part of human life—but I remember being afraid of God. On Sunday mornings, I would come to church and wonder if God would still love me—like the pastor said God would—if God knew how many times I messed up. Sure, I got good grades in school. I listened to my parents and didn't get in trouble with my teachers. But sometimes I got angry. Sometimes I wanted to punch my brother. Even though I tried to have it all together on the outside, I was falling apart on the inside, and I was pretty sure that God wouldn't declare me very good if God saw how hard I had to work to keep myself in one piece.

In college, I was introduced to a skewed idea of total depravity, the idea that humanity was as corrupt as it could be, and to predestination, the belief that God chose before the foundation of the world who was saved and who wasn't. I learned about these ideas and promptly rejected them both. I couldn't believe that God rejected some people before they were born, nor did I want to think that people were as bad as possible, even though it resonated with my own perception of myself. I resisted John Calvin's words: "He who is most deeply abased and alarmed, by the consciousness of his disgrace, nakedness, want, and misery, has made the greatest progress in the knowledge of himself." And yet I wondered if it were true. Was the surest way to know myself to become alarmed by how disgraceful, miserable, and in want I was? It couldn't be. So I pushed Calvinism away. As someone who already struggled to see the good in myself, I didn't need my theology to help me with that. Instead, I decided to tackle my self-doubt by proving to others I was perfect—though I never would have said it that way. I was looking for something external to validate me because I was having trouble finding validation within myself. I threw myself into my schoolwork in the hopes that excelling academically would help me feel like less of a failure inside.

The trouble is, perfectionism doesn't work. None of us are perfect, no matter how hard we try. Perfectionism will either cause us to quit trying to avoid failure preemptively or to run up against the inevitability of failure. Every one of us makes mistakes, and when they happen, our perfectionism cracks and shows itself for the facade that it is. As it breaks, we are left to reckon with what is truly inside of us. "Perfectionism is not about healthy achievement and growth," writes Brené Brown. "Perfectionism is the belief that if we live perfect, look perfect, and act perfect, we can minimize or avoid the pain of blame, judgment, and shame. It's a shield." We turn to perfectionism to shield us from potential pain and shame, but in the process, we cut ourselves off from the goodness God created within us. We cut ourselves off from experiencing the love of God, which does not depend on our ability to earn it.

At our core, we want to be seen and loved. But the entrance of sin into the world did more than make us have to struggle harder for our food; it also made us afraid to be seen for who we are. Adam and Eve's first reaction to having eaten from the tree of the knowledge of good and evil was to hide. They hid not only because they knew what they did was wrong but also because they believed themselves to be shameful. Before the fall, we find this little verse: "And the man and his wife were both naked, and were not ashamed" (Genesis 2:25). In the beginning, they were unashamed. By chapter 3, when God went looking for Adam and Eve, Adam responded, "I heard the sound of you in the garden, and I was afraid, because I was naked; and I hid myself" (Genesis 3:10). In just a matter of verses, the first human beings exchanged their shamelessness for fear and shame. They exchanged the experience of being known and loved for insecurity and secrecy.

As we seek to move with the sacred pulse of appreciation, we must begin by appreciating who we are—people who are created in the image of a good God. We are neither fully perfect nor fully shameful. Though imperfection mars everything in this world, it has not broken the image of

God in us, nor has it repealed the declaration that God made when beholding creation: *Indeed, it was very good.*

Relearning Celebration

As someone well-rehearsed at shame and self-criticism, I need to relearn how to celebrate. In *On Writing*, Stephen King notes that "fear is at the root of most bad writing. . . . Good writing is often about letting go of fear and affectation," affectation being the inclination to define everything we do as "good" or "bad." King says that this need to put everything into a good or bad category is rooted in fear, and we need to let go of that fear in order for creativity and imagination to shine. Although King's words were about writing, they apply more broadly. The first step in relearning how to celebrate is exchanging fear for grace.

Fear is not what we were meant for, "for God did not give us a spirit of cowardice, but rather a spirit of power and of love and of self-discipline." But the passage from 2 Timothy does not end there. It continues, "Do not be ashamed, then, of the testimony about our Lord or of me his prisoner, but join with me in suffering for the gospel, relying on the power of God, who saved us and called us with a holy calling, not according to our works but according to his own purpose and grace" (2 Timothy 1:7–9). When we are not convinced we will be received with love and grace, we can be afraid to let who we are shine. As we relearn celebration, we will also be relearning the love of God, which "casts out fear" (1 John 4:18).

Another obstacle to appreciation and celebration is the seemingly endless nature of much of our work. Before the industrial revolution, the vast majority of people worked in occupations related to agriculture. These jobs were physically active, with tasks that had beginning and end points. Today, far more people work in jobs that require sitting most of the time. An article in the *Journal of the American Heart Association* reports that sedentary jobs have increased 83 percent since 1950. The productivity of these sedentary jobs may be more difficult to quantify because tasks may not always have a tangible end result. In my work as a pastor, I spend a significant amount of time reading and writing. I interact with people. I have conversations. I receive and send emails. Most days, I fall into bed with half-finished projects still in my mind, thinking about the to-do list that is nowhere near completed. When our days are lived to the rhythm and flow of work that is never finished or work that does not have a tangible end result, we can forget to celebrate the work that we have done.

I spent a summer working on the maintenance crew at my seminary. Over the course of that summer, I mowed lawns every week. I mulched the landscaping and painted apartments. Every night before bed, my muscles ached. On lawn mowing days, I was so exhausted I would fall asleep on the couch when I got home. When I went to bed at night, I would think through all of the things I finished that day, and I would feel grateful. The next morning as I walked past all of the lawns I mowed, I took a moment to appreciate the work I had done. I knew exactly how much effort had gone into it, and it filled me with a sense of accomplishment to see the completed work. As a seminary student, I experienced the satisfaction of completing papers and exams, but much of my work didn't have tangible results. I read books, worked at my church internship, and learned how very little I knew (and how much I needed to learn) about matters of faith. My time working in maintenance reinforced to me the value of having something to celebrate.

For those of us who work in career fields or find ourselves in life situations without tangible daily results, it is especially important to find ways to celebrate the work of our hands. This is one reason I took up crocheting and gardening. These hobbies give me something to celebrate and appreciate even when I've had a day when nothing else was finished. Even if the to-do list still had twenty things left on it when I went home in the evening, I could crochet a few rows and see my progress, or I could go out to the garden and pull weeds and see the results. Taking time for celebration is a practice of gratitude that infuses our souls with joy. *The Book of Joy* by the Dalai Lama, Desmond Tutu, and Douglas Abrams talks about the importance of celebration and gratitude in this way: "All things are slipping away, and there is a real danger of wasting our precious human life. Gratitude helps us catalog, celebrate, and rejoice in each day and each moment before they slip through the vanishing hourglass of experience." Those of us skilled at recognizing our failures or at keeping ourselves so busy we don't pause to appreciate the small stuff may need to relearn the art of celebration.

One way to begin relearning celebration and appreciation is by praying the Examen. The Examen is a daily prayer practice that begins with giving thanks. As you begin the prayer, you think back over the course of your day and consider what you are grateful for. The practice of offering prayers of gratitude helps us pause and celebrate the good things in our lives that we might have missed in our busyness. Next in the prayer of Examen, we pray for the Spirit to help us discern where we might have fallen short during the day. We ask for forgiveness. And then we pray for the day to come, that we might approach the new day well. For those of us who have a loud inner critic, it is important that we begin the prayer of Examen by asking for the Holy Spirit's guidance. We do not want our prayer practice to become a time of self-loathing or perfectionism; we want it to be guided by the Spirit who will whisper the truth of our belovedness to us while also gently correcting us where we've made mistakes. Ending our day with appreciation and gratitude helps us to punctuate our lives with celebration.

Everyday Appreciation

Before we finalized our decision to get some backyard chickens, I researched chicken breeds that would do well with the extreme western Nebraska weather. My favorite breed was the Easter Egger. Easter Eggers are a mixed breed chicken, with the possibility of laying blue, green, brown, or even pink eggs. There is no way to know for sure what color egg an Easter Egger will lay until it actually happens, but each hen will lay the same color egg through her laying life. Easter Eggers are tolerant of cold weather and docile, so our kids could help raise them. The downside is that they often take longer to begin laying eggs than other breeds.

In April, I called the local farm store and placed an order for four Easter Egger chicks, which arrived a few weeks later. While they grew, my husband built a chicken coop and run, and my kids took turns helping me feed the chicks. We handled them every day so they would get used to our presence. Once the weather was warm enough, we brought the chickens outside every evening to give them a chance to roam the yard. When they were old enough, we moved them into their coop outside. That first night I don't think I slept at all as I worried about how they would adjust. They did great, and soon our attention turned to excitement. We couldn't wait for them to begin laying, and we wondered what color eggs we might get.

The weather grew colder, and the leaves began changing on the trees. We knew a few people who got chickens the same time we did, and all their chickens were laying. Ours weren't. No big deal. We knew Easter Eggers might take longer. We waited and waited, weeks and weeks, but no eggs. Chickens need at least twelve hours of daylight to lay eggs reliably, and with the changing seasons and forecasted snow, I started to think we might not get eggs until spring. At the end of October, a major snowstorm was predicted, and I declared to my whole family that there would be no eggs until spring. But it was OK. We were having a whole lot of fun with our chickens. They would lay when they were ready, even if it wasn't as soon as we had hoped. We ended up getting a foot of snow, and the overnight temperatures dropped well below zero.

Just as the temperature began to warm back up and the snow started to melt, we hauled some new bedding out to the coop. As we spread the bedding around, we discovered a small, olive-green egg! After waiting so many weeks for our first egg, I was beyond excited to discover it. And how wonderful that it was such a beautiful green! We posed for pictures with our first egg. I took the egg out of the fridge several times just to admire it. I sent pictures of the egg to my family and posted it all over social media. After raising our chickens from little fluff balls into fully grown birds, I realized that eggs were a miracle. How many times had I gone to the grocery store and bought a dozen eggs without even thinking about it? Twelve miracles for a few bucks and almost no effort on my part. Now that I know what goes into raising eggs, I don't think I will ever look at an egg the same way again.

In his commencement speech at Marquette in 2001, Fred Rogers said this about appreciation: "You see, I believe that appreciation is a holy thing, that when we look for what's best in the person we happen to be with at the moment, we're doing what God does. So, in loving and appreciating our neighbor, we're participating in something truly sacred." The busyness and chaos of the world try to urge us to look ahead and beyond what's right in front of us, but appreciation pauses and takes notice. Appreciation is a subversive act of seeing, of knowing. And in pausing to appreciate and celebrate the goodness all around us, I believe that we, too, are seen and known.

We may not think that appreciating ourselves and our work has much to do with appreciating others and the

world around us, but I believe they are related. Appreciation is a muscle we can exercise and strengthen. As we
look at the work of our hands and breathe a grateful sigh
of appreciation, we are training our minds and our hearts
to look for things to celebrate. In Sarah Bessey's beautiful
prayer "A Prayer to Learn to Love the World Again," she
writes, "God of herons and heartbreak, teach us to love the
world again." She goes on to enumerate both the tough and
the beautiful stuff of life, with the repeated call for God to
help us love this world again. In learning to appreciate the
small stuff, we are learning how to love the place where we
are. As we learn to appreciate the small things in our lives
and the small things we have accomplished, we also learn to
love ourselves—the first part of the greatest commandment.
In learning to love ourselves, we strengthen our muscles
for loving our neighbors and for loving and appreciating
the world we inhabit. Appreciation and celebration are a
way of loving what's around and within us, and loving the
One who made it all in the first place.

Our minds so often default to criticism or negativ-
ity. We see problems instead of opportunities. When we
choose to view things negatively rather than positively,
we miss out on so much of the joy of life. When someone
appreciates us, we are motivated to keep on doing the
work. Being appreciated helps us to keep going, and it
encourages us to know that someone else sees what we
do and benefits from it. In the same way, when we express
appreciation for the things we have and for the people we
know, we will share that encouragement, motivation, and
gratitude with others.

Miraculous things surround us daily, but we miss them because of their familiarity. We can reclaim the wonder of ordinary marvels and tap into the sacred pulse of appreciation by living more intentionally. This can look like picking up a hobby that makes a finished product, or it can look like reconnecting to the delightful things that are already in our lives. If you do not have the space to garden, you can still learn about the way food grows. If you do not have a yard to take care of, there are many other ways to get your hands dirty and celebrate the miracle of creation.

When I take my dogs for walks around my neighborhood, I almost always see something unexpected that helps me appreciate where I live. The sun might envelop the bluff and cause the trees to stand out as though they were each hand-painted on a canvas. I might see a bird that I haven't seen before, or hear a bird calling out to others in nearby trees. Sometimes the air smells like spring blossoms or the leaves crunch underfoot. I've even marveled over a brilliantly colored insect I had never seen before. Though I fall captive to self-criticism and perfectionism far more times than I care to admit, immersing myself in the outdoors is one of the quickest ways to be overwhelmed with appreciation and celebration. Learning to appreciate the beautiful things around me helps me strengthen my ability to find things to celebrate in myself and others.

In Genesis 28, Jacob was traveling and stopped to rest for the night. As he slept with his head on a rock for a pillow, he had a dream about the angels of God going up and down a ladder that reached all the way up to heaven. After having the dream, Jacob woke up and declared, "Surely the Lord is in this place—and I did not know it!" Verse 17 continues, "And he was afraid, and said, 'How awesome is this place! This is none other than the house of God, and this is the gate of heaven.'" (Genesis 28:16–17). The day before, Jacob had decided to sleep there because night was falling. He did not recognize the holiness of the place where he laid his head, nor did he recognize the presence of God. It wasn't until he was asleep that God greeted him and shook him out of his inattentiveness. So often we go through the motions in the ordinary stuff of life without a second thought. Meanwhile, God is there with us, and we are too focused to notice. Celebration and appreciation shake us out of our slumber. Perhaps God is appearing to us in this moment, not in a heavenly staircase filled with angels, but in the eggs in our refrigerator, the flowers in the sidewalk cracks, and the kind word that came when we needed it most.

11

REPETITION OF REST
The Holy Rhythm of Restoration

I learned about rest when I collapsed onto the floor of my office—although the word *learned* makes it sound a lot tidier than it was. I had been responding to emails before breaking for lunch when suddenly I felt shaky, restless, and out of breath. My heart was racing, and I felt like I was coming out of my own skin. After ruling everything else out, my doctor told me that I had suffered a panic attack. My body had long been crying out to me for help, and I had become exceptionally skilled at ignoring all its signals. If I wasn't going to take a time-out on my own, my mind and body were going to make it happen for me.

In my office that day, my need for rest hit me like a pickup truck. The problem wasn't that I was behind on taking a day off, though I probably was. It wasn't that I had neglected to get enough sleep or eat nutritious foods, though I'm sure that was part of it. Over the course of the months and years since that experience on the floor of my office, I have learned that what I needed most (along with a good therapist and better sleep and eating habits) was real, restorative rest. Rest, it turns out, doesn't always look like an oversized comforter, extra pillows, and the alarm clock turned off. A day off and a good night's sleep are not the cure for chronic weariness, though time away and sleep are important parts of a healthy routine. Rest is a rhythm that leads to restoration. It means saying no to many things so that we can say yes to what heals, builds, and refreshes.

In the book of Genesis, God creates the world with rhythm and movement. Though each day of God's creative work was different in content, the rhythm of "morning and evening" and the declaration of creation's goodness hold the poetic telling together. The rhythm of the story of creation moves the reader along until we reach a variation in the pattern. Six times throughout the account of creation, we are told that creation was good (the Hebrew word *tov*). This goodness, this well-being, existed between all of the things God created. On the seventh usage of the word *good*, the rhythm changes in a small but significant way. This time, God saw that creation was not only "good"; it was "very good" (*tov me'od*). This "very-goodness" was the wholeness and well-being that God intended for the world (Genesis 1:31). This wholeness was *shalom*.

Lisa Sharon Harper, public theologian and prolific author, notes that while the Greeks saw perfection or goodness as something located within a person or an object itself, the Hebrew people found it *between* things, or *between* people. For the Hebrew people, goodness was not a personal quest for happiness. Instead, goodness looked like the wholeness and completeness of well-being and shalom in all the interconnectedness of the world. "Very good" serves as the punctuation mark, as the indication of completeness and wholeness, and it is after this declaration that God rests from the work of creation. The seventh day was set apart as a blessed day, a hallowed opportunity for rest.

God's act of resting initiated the rhythm of work and rest, creation and appreciation. Citing the work of biblical scholar Terry McGonigal, Harper writes, "The [biblical] writers are communicating the completeness and perfect interconnectedness of the web of creation. It is *tov me'od* because all the relationships between things overflow with goodness!"

Resting in Enough

I remember my Sunday School teacher telling our class God did not rest out of tiredness on the seventh day. After all, how could the God who created everything be tired? She taught us that God rested as an example for us to follow, as a way to show us the importance of rest. I believe this is true, but I also believe there is more to it than that. God rested not only so that we would be reminded to rest but also to show us where rest is found. Restorative rest is not found by never missing a day off. Rest is not found by keeping a set of rules and regulations to prevent us from doing too much. We are not guaranteed to find rest even when we are doing something we enjoy. Rest is found in the acknowledgment of the "very-goodness" of who God has created us to be.

I am terrible at resting—or at least, I didn't learn how to rest until I crashed and burned a few times. Even with these experiences of hard-won wisdom, I still have to remind myself to rest and urge myself not to push it to the wayside. I always thought I struggled with rest because I was driven and goal-oriented, or because I liked crossing things off my to-do list. But the longer I have grappled with finding the rhythm of rest and well-being that God embodied on that first seventh day, the more I have realized the issue goes far deeper. What usually happens when I try to rest goes something like this:

I sit down to rest. Somehow my eyes are drawn to the dirty dishes on the counter. I get up and wash the dishes. After I wash the dishes, I decide to get a snack. I open the refrigerator and realize it needs to be cleaned. The vegetables in the crisper drawer need to be used up, so I decide to make veggie broth. I start the veggie broth, then I decide now is the perfect time to clean out the cabinet with all the Tupperware containers in it. I wonder to myself if there is a reason there are so many more lids than there are containers. And before I know it, I have spent the entire day working away on tasks and projects and accomplishments without pausing for refreshment and restoration.

None of these tasks are bad. The inclination to complete them isn't bad either. The trouble—at least for me—is that even when my body is still, my mind races with everything I need to get done. I used to think this was because I was a go-getter, but I have come to realize my inability to rest hinges on a quiet whisper that tells me I am not enough, that I need to do more to make up for what I lack inside of myself. That little voice within tells me that if I don't wash the dishes in my sink every single night before I go to bed, I have failed. When I put my feet up and take a night off, self-doubt rises up, asking if I've earned the break. The cluttered end table, the unfolded laundry, the stack of thank-you notes to be written—all seem to whisper to me that taking time away is irresponsible. Making sure I take a day off can help ease some of the physical exhaustion. But unless I dig deep and root out the lies that tell me I am *not* very good like God says I am, I will exhaust myself trying to prove I am worthy of love and rest.

After a particularly stressful week, my husband encouraged me and our two kids to sit and watch a movie together on a Friday night. This sounded like a wonderful idea, so I sat down on the couch next to Jeff and reached for my bag of yarn and a crochet hook. I love to crochet while the television is on, so this grasp for my unfinished crochet project was not anything new. This time, however, as I reached for it, I felt a nudge: *Just sit and watch the movie.* I put the yarn and hook down, and I decided to spend some time fully present with my family as we watched the movie together. The movie started, and I was unsettled by how restless I felt as I sat there. My hands started to fidget. My mind wandered to the dishes in the sink, the crochet project at my feet, the deadlines I was behind on. Sitting and watching that movie with my family was *work* for me. A little voice urged me to think of all the things I *should* be doing while watching the movie, all of the *productive* things. As I sat on the couch to watch that movie, I became acutely aware of how possible it is to take time out without really resting. Somewhere along the way, I had convinced myself that I had to earn rest by first finishing everything on my list. Yet the list we make when we are convinced we need to earn our worth is a list that can never be finished.

Hidden beneath our overworking and overfunctioning is often a kernel of self-doubt, a sense of inadequacy. We might be inclined to throw ourselves into our work because we believe our work will give us a sense of purpose. We may immerse ourselves in our hobbies because we hope to find in them a sense of validation. The ways we can overwork and overfunction are as varied as we are, but underneath it all remains the tiny voice asking us if we are good enough just the way we are. We do not look at who God created us to be and find ourselves "very good." At best, we might look at ourselves and see a work-in-progress. At our worst moments, we might look at ourselves and see a big mess that will never be cleaned up. Resting feels like laziness, or like failure, or like we will fall behind in our endless pursuit of showing the world who we are—or who we want to be. We may try to cover up a sense of shame or self-doubt by looking for a sense of meaning or purpose outside of ourselves. We may even convince ourselves that our fixation on what we do is good because it yields a positive outcome. Even very good activities can become very exhausting activities when we do them to convince ourselves and others that we are worthy of being loved.

To say it simply: we are not God. We do not rest to set an example for others to follow. We rest because we need it. Without it, not only does our physical health begin to suffer, but also our mental, emotional, and spiritual well-being. As I sat on that couch with my family, with the movie drowned out by the noise in my own mind, I couldn't run from that self-doubt. Sitting down to rest was an admission that I couldn't do it all, I couldn't be everything to every person, and I had limits. Rather than embracing those human limitations, I wanted to pretend they weren't there.

Resisting Legalism

In a chapter on sleeping, Tish Harrison Warren explains that the Jewish understanding of a day is unlike our Western understanding. For many of us, a day begins with the break of dawn's first light. But in the Jewish understanding, a day begins with the fall of night. The day begins as we move into sleep. She writes this: "This understanding of time is powerfully reorienting, even jarring, to those of us who measure our days by our own efforts and accomplishments. The Jewish day begins in seemingly accomplishing nothing at all. . . . Though the day begins in darkness, God is still at work, growing crops, healing wounds, giving rest, protecting, guarding, mending, redeeming. We drop out of consciousness, but the Holy Spirit remains at work."

True, restorative rest begins with the acceptance of our limitations. But accepting our limitations runs both counter to our instincts and counter to the messages that inundate us every day. When Adam and Eve sinned, their instinct was not to own up but to hide. Deep down, they were afraid of what God would do if they were honest about their shortcomings, and so they decided together it was better to conceal what they had done than to open up and set their failure free. This instinct is still alive and well in us (at least it is in me).

The instinct to hide can manifest itself in our lives as imposter syndrome. Imposter syndrome says that it is only a matter of time before people figure out our weaknesses, our shortcomings. It tells us we don't, in fact, have our lives as put together as we like to pretend. Imposter syndrome is the invisible force that causes much of our procrastination and even our resistance to rest. I resist saying no or setting limits out of fear that others will see my limitations. I worry that if others see my limitations, they will reject me, or they will see me for the imposter I believe myself to be.

Sometimes we resist accepting our limitations because of our instinct to hide our failures; other times we resist accepting them because of social pressure. Some of this pressure is covert. We may take on more tasks at work or say yes to things we don't have the energy for, not because someone has told us we are a failure, but because we see our friends, our coworkers, and our family members juggling everything without apparent effort. We might resist setting up healthy boundaries for ourselves because we are concerned we will appear weak, or lazy, or that we won't measure up. Yet every single human being was created with the need for rest and restoration, even the ones who are juggling too many tasks and wearing too many hats. The fast-paced, breakneck, I-can-do-everything rhythm of many of our communities may encourage us to ignore our need for rest, but the need is still there. We can manage that way for a time—sometimes even for a long time. But eventually, it catches up with us, as it did with me in my office years ago.

In other situations, we may face overt pressure to push boundaries aside and take on more than we can manage. We may be threatened with losing our jobs, missing out on a promotion, or losing face in the community if we do not take on one more project or add one more thing to our heap. While I have often faced covert pressure to ignore the need for rest, that pressure has occasionally moved from covert to overt. Overt pressure can come with high-stakes consequences. Failure to keep saying yes may lead to deep loss, and the fear of that deep loss propels us to continue saying yes even when it costs us dearly.

In the face of these pressures, we face another temptation: the temptation to swing the opposite way and create a legalistic system to prevent ourselves from overwork. In the United States, blue laws were developed as a way to enforce the morality of observing a day of rest. These laws prohibited any activities deemed as "secular" in an effort to maintain the religious observance of a Sunday off. Even after many of these laws fell to the wayside, many denominations and communities maintained rigid expectations for observing a day of rest. A friend told me her parents grew up being told they could not leave the house on Sundays unless they were in their church clothes. Someone might see them outside, and it was important they maintain the appearance of faithful worship attendance. They might have been taking a walk around the neighborhood, but they wanted their neighbors to think they were headed out to church.

When we moved to Holland, Michigan, for seminary, my husband and I went grocery shopping on a Sunday. Our kitchen was still packed up in boxes, but our grill was set up. We decided we'd grill brats, which my husband boils in beer before grilling, only to find out in an embarrassing way that alcohol was not sold on Sundays in that particular community. (That law has since changed, but I still laugh to myself at the way the cashier put the beer off to the side and refused to ring it up.)

Historically, one way Christians have tried to ensure a rhythm of rest is by becoming legalistic about it. When I realized how desperately I needed real, restorative rest, my first instinct was to become rigid too. I would write "day off" on my calendar so that every time someone wanted to meet with me on one of those days off, I would be reminded not to schedule something. I would leave my house first thing in the morning on those days and go somewhere else—usually to a coffee shop or for a walk—to remind myself that the day was supposed to be different. I grew in my ability to say no and to set limits. And this worked for a while. But I felt so guilty when I would take that time away. My mind would wander to what sorts of things I could be accomplishing. Even when I wasn't "on," I felt "on." After a while, I started to both dread days off and feel desperately in need of them. As the dread part grew, I started to let myself slip a little bit. Maybe it wouldn't be so bad for me to go into the office and check my voice mail. That only takes a few minutes. Or maybe I shouldn't count that working lunch as work because it would be fun for me and because I like my church members. I would default on taking time away . . . and then feel guilty for not taking time away.

It turns out that the answer to chronic weariness isn't a rigid day off. The answer isn't legalistic rest, which becomes no rest at all. The answer is contentment. Without contentment, there can be no rest. Without contentment, a day off will not be restorative. Without contentment, laws closing businesses every week will not address the weariness of our souls. Contentment isn't the same as complacency. Contentment isn't settling for less or being comfortable with mediocrity. True contentment that happens inside ourselves makes true rest and restoration possible.

For Rabbi Abraham Joshua Heschel, the rhythm of rest is not about legalism but about the celebration of what God has already done. He says it this way: "To observe the seventh day does not mean merely to obey or to conform to the strictness of a divine command. To observe is to celebrate the creation of the world and to create the seventh day all over again, the majesty of holiness in time." God rested because it was very good. We rest, too, when we discover the contentment that comes from receiving that declaration of "very goodness" for ourselves.

Connecting to Contentment

In Philippians 4, Paul writes about contentment: "I have learned to be content whatever the circumstances" (Philippians 4:11 NIV). The word for contentment in this verse is a Greek word that can also be translated as "self-sufficient."

However, if we merely insert "self-sufficient" into the verse in place of the word *content*, we miss what Paul was communicating to the church. Paul was not saying that he has learned how to be resourceful regardless of the obstacles he faced, or that he didn't need a community or help from anyone else. If we take the idea of self-sufficiency from our Western viewpoint, we will miss the radical statement Paul was making. For Paul, this contentment or self-sufficiency was not something to be achieved by our own strength. We don't arrive at it by pulling ourselves up by our own bootstraps. Contentment is the peace that comes from knowing we have enough in Christ. More than that, contentment is the belief that *we are enough*.

I imagine it was a hard-fought battle for Paul to arrive at the place where he could honestly say he was content—or enough—in all his circumstances. Paul, who had persecuted the early church and worked diligently to quell the movement of The Way (the name given to early Christians), went from a respected observer of the law to an outsider viewed with suspicion. He went from having clout and authority to having to convince members of the early church he could be trusted. As he traveled to spread the news about Jesus, he encountered harrowing situations in which he was persecuted, stoned and left for dead, and imprisoned. Contentment for Paul did not mean ignoring the gravity of his situation. Instead, he had discovered the inner peace that comes from receiving God's declaration of very-goodness. Whether he was honored in prestigious circles or ostracized for who he was, he was beloved by God, and in God's eyes, he was *enough*.

When we rest, we accept the most beautiful gift of all: the truth of our belovedness. To God, we do not cease to be beloved because we did not complete our to-do list. We do not gain our belovedness by overextending ourselves and trying to prove we can do everything. Our belovedness just *is*. It is who we are created to be, and our belovedness exists apart from our efforts. I had spent much of my life either ignoring boundaries in order to please the people around me or setting up rigid boundaries to safeguard the rest and restoration I deeply needed. I have learned, however, that it does not matter how many days off I take or how much sleep I get every night if I do not accept or receive God's declaration that I am very good. Time away is not the same as rest or restoration. Taking time away from the daily grind gives me the opportunity to savor good things and fills my tank enough to keep me moving forward, but until I receive God's good gift of belovedness, finding true rest will be difficult.

To receive the rest of God is to reverse the curse of shame. Lisa Sharon Harper notes that "at its heart, shame is a fear that our failures, our shortcomings, our true selves make us unworthy of connection. The core lie of shame is *I am not enough*." We cannot undo this core lie by busying ourselves to prove ourselves worthy of love or by presenting ourselves a certain way to others. Instead, we shatter this lie by listening to the truth: we are enough. We are enough not because we are perfect or because we've accomplished enough. We are enough because when God created us, God looked at us and declared, "Indeed, it was very good" (Genesis 1:31). It is true because God said so.

Lynne Twist, author and global activist, talks about sufficiency in this way: "Sufficiency isn't two steps up from poverty or one step short of abundance. It isn't a measure of barely enough or more than enough. Sufficiency isn't an amount at all. It is an experience, a context we generate, a declaration, a knowing that there is enough, and that we are enough."

We are enough because of Jesus, who says, "My grace is sufficient for you, for power is made perfect in weakness" (2 Corinthians 12:9). We break away from the cycle of shame and our weary-making pursuit of perfectionism by embracing our limitations and by accepting the declaration from God that indeed, we are very good. Not because we are perfect. Not because we've landed the right job or bought the right stuff. We are enough because God loves us. Where we are weak, our insufficiency meets the sufficiency of God. When we receive this truth, we are caught up in the work of the new creation. Behold, all things are being made new—even us.

12

COUNTERPOINT OF HOLIDAYS

The Holy Rhythm of the Church Year

One Easter morning, I stood on the church lawn. The sun began to crest over the horizon, and I shared these words with the small group who had gathered with me: "Christ is risen!" "Christ is risen indeed!" came their joyful response—the first words of Easter morning. "Alleluia!" we said together, the sleep still heavy in our eyes but the joy full in our hearts.

Those three words—*Christ is risen*—transport me back to that first resurrection morning in my heart every time I hear them. The rhythm of the sacred calendar shapes my life and forms my habits in ways that transcend what happens in the sanctuary. During my years outside of a liturgical congregation, I wondered if following the same rhythm and calendar every year would become rote and old. I have found the opposite to be true. The more I follow the journey of the sacred calendar, the more I enter into the gospel and experience the story of Jesus. In the sacred days of the church year, I remember the steps Jesus walked and the way he lived, and I am challenged to pattern my life after his. In my remembering, I come face-to-face with how often I fall short of what he has called me to do, and I receive again the words of forgiveness and grace that heal my wounded spirit.

The holy days of the church calendar intersect with the daily rhythm of life in a way that can transform us. For most of us, our calendar centers on the work week or the school week. For those of us in church ministry, our schedules revolve around getting ready for worship services every week. We orient ourselves around the tasks we need to complete, the expectations of our bosses, teachers, or parents, or the demands placed on us by others. When we choose to move in step with the rhythm of the holidays—the holy days—of the church year, those other rhythms do not go away. Instead, these movements intersect each other, much like the counterpoint of an intricately composed musical piece. At times, one melody and rhythm might try to outshine another or push the other into the background. But the story of the life of Jesus is always present, intermingling with the daily movements of our lives and calling us to return to our heart melody once again. The sacred pulse of the church calendar is, in the words of Sister Joan Chittister, "the process of coming back year after year to look at what we already know, on one level, but are newly surprised by again and again."

Some of us have grown up with our lives infused by the movement of the church year. Others have grown up leery of ritual and routine, for fear that it would cheapen the gospel stories. Still others of us may not be sure where we stand in relationship to the Christian faith, but we may find ourselves wondering about Jesus from time to time. No matter where we find ourselves, the rhythm of the church calendar invites us to follow in Jesus's footsteps and allow his heart to transform our own. Sarah Bessey said it this way: "Instead of a Hallmark calendar shaping the conversation of the Church (which was my own tradition), moving us from Valentine's Day to Mother's Day to the national holidays, the people of God through the ages have followed their own rhythm, in the world but not of it."

Whether we are aware of it or not, our rhythms and our habits shape our lives. No matter what our religious practice looks like, all of us are moving in step with some kind of rhythm and liturgy. Tish Harrison Warren notes this when she writes, "Therefore, the question is not whether we have a liturgy. The question is, 'What kind of people is our liturgy forming us to be?'"

Little (and Larger) Liturgies

What good is a church liturgy if it shapes our worship services but does not do anything to shape our lives? If the pulse of our sacred days does not reach out and intersect with the daily stuff of our lives, we have compartmentalized our faith to a mere hour a week (or a little bit more

if we include a few extra services throughout the year).
James K. A. Smith says it this way: "The capital-*L* Liturgy
of Sunday morning should generate lowercase-*l* liturgies
that govern our existence throughout the rest of the week."
And I believe that this happens to all of us, whether we
realize it or not.

Our worship habits and rituals shape us. The goal of
the church calendar is "to attune the life of the Christian
to the life of Jesus, the Christ. It proposes, year after year, to
immerse us over and over again into the sense and substance
of the Christian life until, eventually, we become what we
say we are—followers of Jesus all the way to the heart of
God." Whether we follow the church calendar or a more
informal and spontaneous liturgy, the way we worship influences the way we live.

The flipside is also true. The way we live influences the
way we worship. James K. A. Smith continues, "So if we need
to be intentional about the liturgies of Christian worship in
the congregation, we should be equally intentional about the
liturgies of the household." Yet often, these little liturgies
fly under the radar daily, molding us and shaping us largely
without our notice. Tish Harrison Warren undertook a process of examining her daily, little liturgies, and she found this:
"Examining my daily liturgy as *liturgy*—as something that
both revealed and shaped what I love and worship—allowed
me to realize that my daily practices were malforming me,
making me less alive, less human, less able to give and receive
love throughout my day. Changing this ritual allowed me to
form a new repetitive and contemplative habit that pointed
me toward a different way of being in the world."

The give-and-take between our worship and our daily lives should challenge us to reflect on both the capital-*L* and lowercase-*l* liturgies to ensure that these habits are shaping and forming us in ways that are giving us life.

Laundry is a liturgy. It needs to be done. It's never finished. (And if you put it off long enough, you soon have nothing to wear.) The habitual rhythm of washing, drying, folding, and putting away clothes shapes us into who we are, whether we realize it or not. I'm not the main laundry-doer in my house, but when I spend time doing laundry, I remember that simple, ordinary tasks shape my life every day. Doing the laundry both reveals and molds who I am, as I care for the clothing I wear and the clothing my family wears. As I do laundry, I have to be intentional. Checking the pockets on each pair of pants gives me space to reflect on the way I've spent my week. Laundry helps me to practice patience. The washing machine and the dryer take as long as they take, and they can't be rushed. Folding the laundry invites me to be thankful for the things I have, and it reminds me of the importance of showing love to myself and to my family. (Get some new socks. You need them.) Often without our knowledge, the little liturgies of our days, like laundry, are working on us in ways that shape the way we worship.

Similarly, the way we worship shapes our daily habits—at least, it should. In my theological tradition, a worship service has a three-part structure: Approaching God, Word and Sacrament, and Responding to God. The offering is placed near the end of the service because the giving of our gifts is seen as an act of gratitude rather than an obligation.

This weekly habit of giving as a grateful response shapes the way I view giving in general. When I find myself in a position to give something to someone else—whether it's money or something else—I view that giving as a grateful response to all God has given me. Giving is a free act of thankfulness rather than a duty that leaves me feeling resentful. The weekly practice of giving also helps me free myself from holding too tightly to my material possessions. As Chuck DeGroat writes, "Giving actually helps us to detach ourselves from those things we've been clinging to, to hold our possessions more loosely, and to trust a bit more."

Our little liturgies and our more formal liturgies work to move us either toward the sacred pulse or away from it. Sometimes they work in harmony. Other times we try to compartmentalize our liturgies, keeping them away from one another, and we end up stuck in the middle in a kind of liturgical tug-of-war. What's important is that we realize our liturgies are not neutral—neither the liturgies of our worship nor the little liturgies of daily living. Everything we do is also doing something to us. As we reflect on our liturgies, we may find ourselves in the middle of a liturgical renewal: retaining some liturgies and changing up others. Our daily habits, our liturgies of shopping and grief, friendship and snow days—these all have the potential to draw us into the song of God, the rhythm and pulse that gives life. They also have the potential to distract and disorient us instead. Where our liturgies are moving us away from wholeness and *shalom*—whether our little liturgies or our larger ones—we have the opportunity to exchange them for something that will breathe peace upon our over-whelmed souls.

When Seasons Collide

The four weeks leading up to Christmas in the church year make up the season of Advent. During this season, we wait with anticipation for the coming of Jesus into the world. We light the Advent candles, and we talk about hope, peace, joy, and love. But as anyone who has stepped foot in a major retail store the day after Halloween knows, the Christmas season outside of the church begins November 1. As soon as the trick-or-treaters have gone to bed on Halloween night, the ghosts and ghouls are replaced with Christmas lights and holiday music on every radio station. While the church talks about waiting, listening, and anticipating, flyers come in the mail and ads pop up everywhere, urging us to "buy it now" so we can get into the holiday spirit. One of the delights—and one of the tensions—of following the sacred calendar is that sometimes seasons collide in ways that conflict and challenge us.

My children have two parents who are pastors. This can make the season extra busy at our house as we prepare for school Christmas parties and extra services at church. Almost every Advent sermon I heard growing up focused on the importance of slowing down, breathing deeply, and not falling prey to the commercialism of the secular Christmas season. After becoming a pastor, I preached these sermons too. But I quickly realized something: if I wasn't going to slow down and breathe deeply as I tried to keep up with both the religious observance of Christmas and the secular celebration of it, I probably shouldn't ask the folks in the pews to do it either.

As I was caught between the tension of Advent and commercial Christmas, I started leaning into the themes of each Advent week—hope, peace, joy, and love—and making space to embrace those themes in the midst of Christmas chaos. While this practice didn't magically make all of the stress and busyness of Christmastime go away, it encouraged me to explore the busyness in light of the pace of Advent. It helped me give myself permission to let some things go, and it helped me to better understand the disconnect I was feeling between worship on Sunday mornings and the rest of the days in the month of December. The collision of seasons helped me examine my priorities and begin to move toward a rhythm and a pace that was healthy and sustainable. What good is Christmas joy if you are too exhausted to appreciate it?

The church calendar also gave me another unexpected Christmas gift: the twelve days of Christmas. Christmas celebrations outside of the church usually begin in November and end by December 26. The twelve days of Christmas mark the days between Christmas and Epiphany, January 6. I have found that these twelve days are a perfect time for embracing Christmas without the pressure of gift-giving and parties. While many people have packed Christmas away into boxes and totes for another year, I find myself finally able to rest in the miracle of God made flesh. The extra church services are over. The parties are finished.

The Christmas music has disappeared from the stores. It is amazing to me how I am more fully able to enter into the spirit of Christmas when I am not bombarded by Christmas everywhere I turn. On Epiphany, we bake a three kings cake and hide a baby Jesus figurine inside. We tell the story of the wise men who had gone in search of Jesus, and we see who finds the baby Jesus in their slice of cake. In those precious days after Christmas, after all the cards have been sent, the gifts opened, and the expectations lightened, I find myself better able to ponder the mystery of the incarnation.

The rhythms of daily life can be overwhelming. Their song and rhythm can drown out the quiet places and make it difficult for us to listen to the voice of God. The sacred pulse of holy days helps us tune our ears to the counterpoint melody that has been there all along. Sister Joan Chittister reflects on the way the celebration of the sacred calendar can reorient us: "Like the voices of loved ones gone before us, the liturgical year is the voice of Jesus calling to us every day of our lives to wake our sleeping selves from the drowsing effects of purposelessness and meaninglessness, materialism and hedonism, rationalism and indifference, to attend to the life of the Jesus who cries within us for fulfillment."

The sacred calendar does not erase the breakneck pace of life, nor does it serve as a substitute for the daily calendar of the work and school week. It is not a replacement but a counterpoint melody that sometimes intersects with and sometimes diverges from the melody of our world. The melody of sacred days rings in our ears and changes the way we hear the world's song.

The Widening of Time

We can become so enmeshed in the busyness—the endless lists and the frantic pace of life—that we develop tunnel vision. When we look ahead only far enough to the next task or the next obligation, we can miss the fleeting glimmers of grace, love, and mercy that are all around us. The church year bumps up against the daily expectations and busyness and disorients us just enough that we can widen our view. The holy days and sacred moments interrupt the *chronos* time of our daily lives and urge us to look for the *kairos* moments all around us. The sacred days on the church calendar are not *kairos* moments in themselves—though sometimes they can be—but they open our eyes to the presence of the *kairos* moments we are given every day.

Frederick Buechner once wrote, "Listen to your life. See it for the fathomless mystery it is. In the boredom and pain of it, no less than in the excitement and gladness: touch, taste, smell your way to the holy and hidden heart of it, because in the last analysis all moments are key moments, and life itself is grace." The little moments, the little liturgies of our lives, are where the *kairos* moments happen. We look for God in the sanctuary, but we forget to look in the simple and ordinary, even though the holy is certain to be found there.

On Ash Wednesday, we conclude the worship service with the imposition of ashes. One by one, people come forward and receive a cross of ashes on their foreheads. As the ashes are imposed, these words are spoken: "Remember, you are dust and to dust you shall return." My husband

and I impose the cross of ashes on each other's foreheads, which humbles me every year. Typically, when the service is over and everyone has gone home, I go home and wash the ashes off while praying this prayer: "God, wash away my sin and help me live like your child." But on one particular Ash Wednesday, my kids had a school activity right after the service. Without even thinking about it, we stopped to pick up food from a restaurant and I still had the cross of ashes on my forehead. A few people stared at me as I picked up our meal to go, and I had no idea why. We ate our food and headed to the school event. At the event, people turned their heads to look at us as we walked past. Suddenly I realized the cross of ashes was still on my forehead. I felt self-conscious. I wanted to go wash it off, but I couldn't.

Waiting for the event to begin, I started thinking about how much I'd like to wash off my mortality too. I thought about the times I had let down friends and family, the times when my imperfections were on display. There I sat in my seat, with people glancing at me as they walked past, and I felt vulnerable, which seems perfect for Ash Wednesday. The ashes themselves didn't change me, but receiving them reminded me of my need for change. Ordinary ashes widened my vision to see the *kairos* moment in front of me. My mortality was always true. My imperfections, my missteps, my needs for forgiveness and grace were always reality. I had just allowed myself to forget those things as I lived my busy, chaotic life. In doing so, I also allowed myself to forget the gifts of grace and love that are always being offered to me. In the frenetic pace of my *chronos* life, I had forgotten the reality of the opportune, of the sacred, of the *kairos* moments that are sprinkled throughout each day. In that moment, the ordinariness of my life was widened, and I could see what had always been true but that I had just become skilled at ignoring.

The sacred days of the church calendar are gifts that widen our eyes and widen our experience of time. When the ordinary and the extraordinary intersect, I find myself praying along with Saint Hildegard of Bingen: "I stretch out my hands to God that I might be sustained by Him, just as a feather lacking all force of its own strength flies upon the wind." As the holy days of the church year and the daily stuff of life meet, I am reminded in a new way of my dependence upon the all-embracing love of God. In Psalm 31, the psalmist faced disaster. He prayed, "But I trust in you, O Lord; I say, 'You are my God.' My times are in your hand; deliver me from the hand of my enemies and persecutors. Let your face shine upon your servant; save me in your steadfast love" (Psalm 31:14–16). The writer of Psalm 31 was in grave danger, and yet his eyes were opened to the reality of God's steadfast love. I do not believe the psalm writer had greater faith than any of us might have. If the psalms teach us little else, they should make it clear that we can offer all of who we are—doubts and all—to God.

The psalm writer lived a life centered on the story of the steadfast love of God. In worship, the psalmist would have heard the story, recited the story, prayed the story, and celebrated the story. In prayer, the psalmist rehearsed the story of the goodness of God until his life moved in step with it. Because of this, even in the midst of difficult times, the psalmist asked to see God's goodness—not because the psalmist didn't doubt or struggle, but because the psalm-ist's life had been formed and molded by the story of who God is.

All of us are shaped by the stories we tell (and hear) and by the habits we engage in. The stories we tell and the habits we live by are not neutral. They express what is important to us, and they work on us and change us. When these stories run contrary to the rhythm of God's stories, we become a people off balance and out of rhythm. The church year was put together as an intentional method of reciting and rehearsing the stories of our faith in a way that shapes us into people who live more like Jesus. Even for those who do not follow the church year, the rhythm of holidays is a vibrant way for church bodies, families, and individuals to connect to the sacred pulse that restores our lives. From celebrating the birth of Christ to the shouts of "Alleluia" on Easter morning, the stories and practices of these sacred days remind us that God's story is intersecting with our own stories. Embracing the sacred pulse of holy days allows us to reorient our stories around God's story, and in God's story find the fullness of our own lives.

Over the course of my life, I have fallen out of step with the sacred pulse that brings wholeness and life many times. Whether I've simply skipped a beat or found myself march-ing in step with a whole different rhythm, I have found myself drawn back time and again to the rhythm that heals and restores. Sometimes I still feel like the child sitting on my grandparents' piano bench listening to the metronome and imagining what the song sounds like when put to the beat. And even though I am tempted to do things my own way, I have found that the more I listen to the sacred rhythm, the more it calls out to me when I walk away. This sacred pulse aims to "keep our lives riveted on one beam of light called the death and Resurrection of Jesus and its meaning for us here and now," writes Sister Joan Chittister. Hour by hour, even moment by moment, we are invited to listen and to allow our lives to be reoriented to the story and the pulse that brings life into our weary souls. We can exchange the pace that overwhelms us for the peace that "surpasses all understanding" (Philippians 4:7).

In the middle of writing this book, my life was upended by the COVID-19 pandemic and the deaths of my grandfather and my great-uncle. These experiences have forced me beyond the superficial understanding of God's sacred pulse that I first had in mind when I sat down to write. I was thrust into a way of life in which comfort, routine, and security were taken away. Even though this journey has been painful and disorienting, it has also helped me to find the courage to dive deeper and explore what it means to live my life in step with the life-giving rhythms of God's way, whether my life is going according to plan or everything is falling apart at the seams.

It is my prayer that somewhere within these words you will find the voice of Jesus's steadfast love calling out to you. This voice is the one inviting you to dance, to sing, to create, and to let fall away whatever crushes these beautiful things in you. Though the sacred pulse may sound far away or unfamiliar, we can reconnect to the life-giving pulse in the simple and ordinary stuff of our days. We can listen again to the divine song as we pull up a seat at our tables, as the snow wipes our calendars clean, and when we talk to a neighbor across the backyard fence. Listening again for the rhythm doesn't need to be complicated. It's as simple as beginning again when we open our eyes each new morning.

Even here, even now, in the midst of whatever you may be experiencing, there is still another way.

ACKNOWLEDGMENTS

In many ways, a book is like a garden. We admire the finished product, but none of it would have been possible without good soil, favorable weather, a seed faithfully planted, and a whole lot of old-fashioned, hard work. I am grateful to God for the seed for this book, a peculiar idea about the sacred pulse that invites all of us to dance. Whenever I allowed myself to dream about writing my first book, I had no idea that this would be what I would be called to write about. Words fail to describe my gratitude for Broadleaf Books for taking a chance on a new author like me, and for my editors Elisabeth Ivey and Valerie Weaver-Zercher, who nurtured my tender seedling and encouraged it to grow toward the sun.

The people of the First Presbyterian Church of Scottsbluff, Nebraska, bless me every day with the opportunity to be their pastor. I am thankful to each of them for their encouragement, for their prayers, and for the way they love my family. Without your kindness and encouragement, I would never have had the courage to write this book.

Tim Fall and Jeannie Prinsen helped me pull a lot of weeds. Maranda Coop, my weekly Text Study group and my Thursday morning group, Traci Rhoades, Lisa Deam,

Kristin Kobes Du Mez, Chuck DeGroat, Bronwyn Lea, Anna-Kate Howell, Rob Dixon, Liz Testa, Rae Whitney, Matt Rawle, Aretha Grant, Inés McBryde, and so many others nourished the dry, parched ground when it needed it most.

My #Squad, Matthew van Maastricht and Nick Scutari: you kept this gardener on task (and sometimes distracted from it) in all the best ways. I truly don't know where I would have been throughout this last year without your care, your prayers, and your memes.

My parents, Tim and Kathy Emick: you always encouraged my writing, and anything else I set my mind to. Your care and love for me enabled me to cultivate creativity and a love for the world around me. Thank you. My in-laws, Roger and Sharon Fiet: you love me and welcome me into your family in ways that bless me beyond words. I'm so thankful for you.

My sister-in-law, Becky Fiet: in the midst of a global pandemic, when everything was falling apart, you still made time to listen to me, to urge me not to give up, and to help me laugh when I needed that more than anything. My brother, Zach, and my sister-in-law, Debra Emick: I am grateful for you and for the ways you demonstrate to me love, compassion, hard work, and grace.

To my whole family, I love you more than words can say. Thank you for who you are.

I think God gave me the seed to plant about the sacred pulse of God's life-giving rhythm because I am an expert at straying from it. To my husband, Jeff: I am so grateful for the way you helped me keep our home in balance while I wrote, for the way you love our children, for the mugs of chai you made me when I was elbow-deep in revisions, and for always sending me the right GIF when I needed it. Jakob and Malia, this book would not have been possible without your curiosity and imagination. You inspire me every day. You both have a way of showing up by my writing desk when I most need a hug, of reminding me to take a break and look around me, and of keeping me laughing. You are both growing into such amazing people. I'm proud to be your mom.

My dogs, Wishbone and Pippy, supplied me with the snuggles and outdoor walks I needed to stay healthy and happy. My backyard chickens gave me an excuse to get outside every day. They are silly enough to remind me not to take myself too seriously. The beautiful western Nebraska skies and the backdrop of the Scotts Bluff National Monument fill my eyes and my heart daily with inspiration. I cannot imagine living anywhere more beautiful.

This book is the fruit of all of the above and more. And now, dear reader, as it is in your hands, I want to express my thanks to you too. You are a part of the growing process of this seed that has become this book. My prayer is that some of these words will find root in your heart. Tend them well. And may they bless you as they grow.

DISCUSSION AND REFLECTION QUESTIONS

Chapter 1: Drumbeat of Time

1. What do you think the psalmist means when he asks God to "teach us to count our days that we may gain a wise heart"?
2. What are the biggest time-wasters in your life? How might you reclaim that time?
3. Where in your life have you been choosing distraction over presence?

Chapter 2: Symphony of the Seasons

1. Have you ever tried growing your own food? If so, how has it changed your perspective on food? If you haven't, why not?
2. How would you rate yourself in terms of your patience level (on a scale of one to ten with one being extremely impatient and ten being extremely patient)? How do you feel about that rating?

3. What is one way you could "get your hands dirty" and reconnect with the rhythm of the seasons?

Chapter 3: Cadence of the Kitchen

1. What are your mealtime rituals? How have those rituals shaped your life?
2. In what ways is eating with someone an act of vulnerability?
3. What distractions do you face at mealtime that can keep you from interacting with those eating with you?

Chapter 4: Tempo of Transactions

1. Think of a time when you had an interaction with someone while you were shopping that made the shopping experience more meaningful to you. What was special about that interaction?
2. What are the biggest barriers to local shopping for you?
3. What is one change you can make to your shopping habits to make them more community-focused?

Chapter 5: Composition of Making

1. "When we are creative—whether in an artistic endeavor or in the way we approach problem-solving— we are living more fully into who we are as people

created in God's image." In what ways do you express your creativity?

2. How has your own creativity or the creativity of others been a light in the darkness for you?

3. What holds you back from being creative?

Chapter 6: Breath Mark of Snow Days

1. Make a list in your mind or on paper of the expectations you have for yourself or that others have for you. What would happen if you let go of these expectations?

2. This chapter describes the difficulty of embracing snow days. What sorts of interruptions to daily life do you find the most difficult to deal with?

3. "What opportunities for beautiful moments exist right here and now, things we would have missed out on if life kept moving the way we had expected?" Think of a time when your schedule was unexpectedly cleared. What beautiful moments were you able to experience that you would have missed out on otherwise?

Chapter 7: Movement of Community

1. What are some ways you could seek out opinions different from your own? Are there any authors, speakers, or people in your daily life who have helped you do this?

2. Which is more difficult for you: giving or receiving? Why do you think that is?

3. Name some obstacles to meaningful social connection that you face. How might you begin to overcome these?

Chapter 8: Harmony of Friendship

1. On a scale of one to ten (with one being not at all comfortable and ten being very comfortable), how comfortable are you spending time alone? What keeps you from feeling comfortable alone? What do you enjoy about being alone?

2. What is an area of your life where you struggle to show yourself compassion? How might you be a better friend to yourself in this area?

3. When have you experienced mutuality in friendship? What was that like?

Chapter 9: Requiem of Grief

1. What words do you associate with failure?

2. Do you have a favorite psalm? If you do, what about this psalm makes it your favorite? Consider writing your own psalm to express both your joys and your griefs.

3. "If we do not accept our griefs, we do not accept ourselves." Do you agree with this? Why or why not?

Chapter 10: Crescendo of Celebration

1. Are you a perfectionist? Whether you are a perfectionist or not, how does your view of yourself impact your view of God?
2. Do you have a difficult time quantifying or measuring the work you do each day or week? How does that impact your ability to celebrate?
3. What are some "small things" you could celebrate right now?

Chapter 11: Repetition of Rest

1. What makes it difficult for you to rest? What can you do to break through these obstacles?
2. What would true, restorative rest look like for you?
3. How would it feel if someone said to you, "You are enough just as you are"?

Chapter 12: Counterpoint of Holidays

1. What rituals or holiday traditions did you grow up with? How did the traditions you grew up with influence who you are?
2. What "little liturgies" are a part of your daily life? How do these "little liturgies" have an impact on the way you worship God?
3. What is a story that you tell often, and how does that story shape your world?

NOTES

Introduction

2 **"humanity chose its own way"**: Lisa Sharon Harper, *The Very Good Gospel: How Everything Wrong Can Be Made Right* (Colorado Springs: WaterBrook, 2016), 47.

9 **"The future will belong"**: Richard Louv, *The Nature Principle: Reconnecting with Life in a Virtual Age* (Chapel Hill, NC: Algonquin, 2012), 4–5.

Chapter 1: Drumbeat of Time

15 **"The psalmist recognizes"**: Walter Brueggemann, *Materiality as Resistance: Five Elements for Moral Action in the Real World* (Louisville, KY: Westminster John Knox, 2020), 66.

17 **"Many of the first Christians"**: Justo González, *A Brief History of Sunday: From the New Testament to the New Creation* (Grand Rapids, MI: Eerdmans, 2017), 39.

17 **"How we spend our days"**: Annie Dillard, *The Writing Life* (New York: HarperCollins, 2007), 31.

18   **"In one report, four out of five":** International Data
      Corporation (IDC), *Always Connected: How Smart-*
      phones and Social Keep Us Engaged, 2013, https://tinyurl
      .com/2unwk6zb.

19   **"Sadly, human beings are":** Matthew Walker, *Why We*
      Sleep: Unlocking the Power of Sleep and Dreams (New York:
      Scribner, 2017), 9.

20   **"Each of us has a master clock":** National Institute
      of General Medical Sciences, "Circadian Rhythms,"
      October 2020, https://tinyurl.com/3dsvbwea.

20   **"The stimulation of light":** Susan Ayers et al., *Cam-*
      bridge Handbook of Psychology, Health and Medicine
      (Cambridge: Cambridge University Press, 2007), 497.

21   **"It is worth noting that":** Brueggemann, *Materiality as*
      Resistance, 63–64.

22   **"Both man and master in the night":** "John O'Dreams,"
      vinyl, track B5 on Bill Caddick, *Rough Music*, Park
      Records, 1976. Based on a tune from Pyotr Ilyich Tchai-
      kovsky's Symphony no. 6, "Pathetique."

25   **"These changes sometimes create":** Hartmut Rosa, *Social*
      Acceleration: A New Theory of Modernity, trans. Jonathan
      Trejo-Mathys (New York: Columbia University Press,
      2013), 68–69.

27   **"Behind every screen":** Hilary Andersson, "Social
      Media Apps Are 'Deliberately' Addictive to Users,"
      BBC News, July 3, 2018, https://www.bbc.com/news/
      technology-44640959.

Chapter 2: Symphony of the Seasons

32 **"In one survey, about 7 percent":** Nancy Coleman, "Chocolate Milk Definitely Doesn't Come from Brown Cows—but Some Adults Think Otherwise," CNN, June 16, 2017, https://tinyurl.com/yryzpsnm.

32 **"According to the USDA, Americans":** USDA Economic Research Service, *Apples and Oranges Are America's Favorite Fruits*, 2018, https://tinyurl.com/hkjbzju6; USDA Economic Research Service, *Potatoes and Tomatoes Are the Most Commonly Consumed Vegetables*, 2019, https://tinyurl.com/2n8k688u.

32 **"A child in upper elementary school":** Alexander J. Hess and Cary J. Trexler, "A Qualitative Study of Agricultural Literacy in Urban Youth: What Do Elementary Students Understand about the Agri–Food System?," *Journal of Agricultural Education* 52, no. 4 (2011): 7, https://tinyurl.com/22hm3cc9.

33 **"In the early 1800s":** These statistics come from the following: Stanley Lebergott, "Labor Force and Employment, 1800–1960," in *Output, Employment, and Productivity in the United States after 1800*, ed. Dorothy S. Brady (Cambridge, MA: National Bureau of Economic Research, 1966), https://tinyurl.com/dkc3w3pp; USDA Economic Research Service, "Farm Labor," updated April 22, 2020, https://tinyurl.com/smetz43x; and USDA Economic Research Service, "Ag and Food Sectors and the Economy," updated December 16, 2020, https://tinyurl.com/3pwuppz2.

35   **"Most eaters . . . think of food":** Wendell Berry, *What Are People For? Essays* (Berkeley, CA: Counterpoint, 2010), 153–54.

36   **"In the United States, we have":** NASA Earth Observatory, "More Lawns Than Irrigated Corn," November 8, 2005, https://tinyurl.com/rz3vbt3c.

Chapter 3: Cadence of the Kitchen

53   **"Isn't a meal together":** Henri J. M. Nouwen, *The Life of the Beloved: Spiritual Living in a Secular World* (Chestnut Ridge, NY: Crossroad, 2002), 110.

57   **"80 percent of all dinners":** NPD Group, "U.S. Consumers Are Increasingly Eating and Preparing Their Meals at Home Often with the Help of Foodservice," July 24, 2018, https://tinyurl.com/hnkmdrf9.

58   **"loneliness as a silent health crisis":** Vivek H. Murthy, *Together: The Healing Power of Human Connection in a Sometimes Lonely World* (New York: HarperCollins, 2020), xv.

59   **"At the Last Supper Jesus":** Tish Harrison Warren, *Liturgy of the Ordinary: Sacred Practices in Everyday Life* (Downers Grove, IL: InterVarsity, 2016), 63.

60   **"We eat from the one loaf":** Jill J. Duffield, *Lent in Plain Sight: A Devotion through Ten Objects* (Louisville, KY: Westminster John Knox, 2020), 37–38.

Chapter 4: Tempo of Transactions

69 **"The word *convenience*":** *Merriam-Webster*, s.v. "convenient," accessed February 21, 2021, https://www.merriam-webster.com/dictionary/convenient.

74 **"Something like 87 percent":** Ruomeng Cui et al., "Sooner or Later? Promising Delivery Speed in Online Retail," ResearchGate, April 2020, https://tinyurl.com/3jkp23cf.

75 **"The woman made 77 cents":** William T. Cavanaugh, *Being Consumed: Ethics and Christian Desire* (Grand Rapids, MI: Eerdmans, 2008), 26.

78 **"Extracting money":** Brueggemann, *Materiality as Resistance*, 15.

80 **"Jesus does not teach":** Justo L. González, *Luke: Belief, a Theological Commentary on the Bible* (Louisville, KY: Westminster John Knox, 2010), 211.

Chapter 5: Composition of Making

86 **"To say that I am made":** Thomas Merton, *New Seeds of Contemplation* (Cambridge, MA: New Directions, 2007), 60.

87 **"The discipline of creation":** Madeleine L'Engle, *Walking on Water: Reflections on Faith and Art* (New York: Convergent, 2016), 61.

88 **"another way of being human":** Frederick Buechner, *The Longing for Home: Reflections at Midlife* (New York: HarperCollins, 2009), 110.

91 **"I write to find out":** Stephen King, *The Colorado Kid* (New York: Simon & Schuster, 2005), 184.

91 **"When we sit down":** Steven Pressfield, *The War of Art: Break through the Blocks and Win Your Inner Creative Battles* (New York: Black Irish Entertainment, 2002), 108.

92 **"Those of us who write":** Andrew Peterson, *Adorning the Dark: Thoughts on Community, Calling, and the Mystery of Making* (Nashville: B&H, 2019), 123.

93 **"All children are artists":** L'Engle, *Walking on Water*, 43.

94 **"Perfectionism is the voice":** Anne Lamott, *Bird by Bird: Some Instructions on Writing and Life* (New York: Anchor, 1995), 28.

95 **"You think you belong":** Shahran Shiva, *Hush, Don't Say Anything to God: Passionate Poems of Rumi* (Fremont, CA: Jain, 2000), 31.

Chapter 6: Breath Mark of Snow Days

101 **"Clay is shaped to make":** Lao Tzu, *Tao Te Ching: A New Translation*, trans. Sam Hamill (Boston: Shambhala, 2007), 15.

102 **"But in those moments":** Brené Brown, *Rising Strong: How the Ability to Reset Transforms the Way We Live, Love, Parent, and Lead* (New York: Random House, 2017), xxv.

107 **"Dear God, I so much want":** Henri J. M. Nouwen, *With Open Hands* (Notre Dame, IN: Ave Maria, 2005), 61.

110 **"making a shift in her life":** Marie Kondo, *The Life-Changing Magic of Tidying Up: The Japanese Art of*

Decluttering and Organizing (New York: Ten Speed Press, 2014), 41.

111 **"grace fills empty spaces":** Simone Weil, *Gravity and Grace* (Lincoln: University of Nebraska Press, 1997), 55.

111 **"as a ribbon of mountain air":** Anne Lamott, *Small Victories: Spotting Improbable Moments of Grace* (New York: Riverhead, 2014), 183.

Chapter 7: Movement of Community

118 **"When you are born":** Kaitlin Curtice, *Native: Identity, Belonging, and Rediscovering God* (Grand Rapids, MI: Brazos, 2020), xi.

118 **"No matter who we are":** Curtice, 12.

120 **"These days, Christians can":** Christena Cleveland, *Disunity in Christ: Uncovering the Hidden Forces That Keep Us Apart* (Downers Grove, IL: InterVarsity, 2013), 26–27.

124 **"satisfaction of helping":** Larry Dossey, "The Helper's High," *Explore* 14, no. 6 (2018): 393–99.

124 **"Our strategy needs":** M. Scott Peck, *The Different Drum: Community-Making and Peace* (New York: Touchstone, 2010), 233.

126 **"Until we can receive":** Brené Brown, *The Gifts of Imperfection: Let Go of Who You Think You're Supposed to Be and Embrace Who You Are* (Center City, MN: Hazelden, 2010), 20.

127 **"In our individualized society":** John Donne, *Devotions: Upon Emergent Occasions* (Ann Arbor: University of Michigan Press, 1959), 108–9.

129 **"So the challenge today":** Chuck DeGroat, *Wholeheart-edness: Busyness, Exhaustion, and Healing the Divided Self* (Grand Rapids, MI: Eerdmans, 2016), 186.

129 **"trend of social disconnection":** Murthy, *Together*, 156.

Chapter 8: Harmony of Friendship

135 **"place in the family":** Mary Oliver, "Wild Geese," in *Dream Work* (New York: Atlantic Monthly, 1986), 14.

136 **"the word *loneliness*":** Murthy, *Together*, 58.

137 **"a study that shows":** Warren, *Liturgy of the Ordinary*, 33.

138 **"the creation of an open":** Richard Foster and Julia Roller, *A Year with God: Living Out the Spiritual Disciplines* (New York: HarperOne, 2009), 185.

138 **"Settle yourself in solitude":** Teresa of Ávila, quoted in Richard J. Foster, *Celebration of Discipline: The Path to Spiritual Growth* (New York: HarperCollins, 1988), 96.

139 **"all of humanity's problems":** Blaise Pascal, quoted in Maartje Willems, *The Lost Art of Doing Nothing: How the Dutch Unwind with Niksen* (New York: Experiment, 2021), 28.

141 **"The fog of loneliness":** Murthy, *Together*, 194–95.

142 **"The elusive wholeness":** DeGroat, *Wholeheartedness*, 160–61.

143 **"lowest [despair] of all":** Søren Kierkegaard, *Sickness Unto Death* (London: Start, 2012), 55.

145 **"Unfortunately, many people confuse":** Murthy, *Together*, 217.

Chapter 9: Requiem of Grief

150   **"the book that gave us":** Elisabeth Kübler-Ross, *On Death and Dying: What the Dying Have to Teach Doctors, Nurses, Clergy, and Their Own Families* (London: Routledge, 2009), 2.

152   **"a conference on failure":** Brown, *Rising Strong*, xxvi.

156   **"Pretending that things":** Anne Lamott, *Stitches: A Handbook on Meaning, Hope, and Repair* (New York: Riverhead, 2013), 40.

157   **"raging torrent of grief":** J. Todd Billings, *Rejoicing in Lament: Wrestling with Incurable Cancer and Life in Christ* (Grand Rapids, MI: Brazos, 2015), 47.

158   **"As Billings grappled":** Billings, 47.

160   **"griefs not as temporary losses":** Nora McInerny, "We Don't Move on from Grief. We Move Forward with It," TED video, 2018, https://tinyurl.com/2w9rfm5k.

161   **"The stages of grief have evolved":** Elisabeth Kübler-Ross, *On Grief and Grieving: Finding the Meaning of Grief through the Five Stages of Loss* (New York: Scribner, 2014), 7.

162   **"Grant me that I may":** Rabindranath Tagore, *Fruit Gathering* (New York: Macmillan, 1916), lxxix, https://tinyurl.com/yhec34h5.

Chapter 10: Crescendo of Celebration

167 **"God gave a loaf":** Emily Dickinson, "Enough," in *Selected Poems: Unabridged* (New York: Dover, 1990), 38.

171 **"He who is most deeply":** John Calvin, *Institutes of the Christian Religion*, trans. Henry Beveridge (Grand Rapids, MI: Christian Classics Ethereal Library, 1845), 231.

171 **"Perfectionism is not":** Brown, *Gifts of Imperfection*, 56.

173 **"fear is at the root":** Stephen King, *On Writing: A Memoir of the Craft* (New York: Scribner, 2010), 127–28.

174 **"Another obstacle to appreciation":** James A. Levine, "Lethal Sitting: Homo Sedentarius Seeks Answers," *Physiology* 29, no. 5 (September 2014): 300–301, https://tinyurl.com/bsh4vsjm.

174 **"sedentary jobs have increased":** Allene L. Gremaud et al., "Gamifying Accelerometer Use Increases Physical Activity Levels of Sedentary Office Workers," *Journal of the American Heart Association*, July 2, 2018, https://tinyurl.com/y84f92p3.

175 **"All things are slipping away":** Dalai Lama, Desmond Tutu, and Douglas Abrams, *The Book of Joy: Lasting Happiness in a Changing World* (New York: Avery, 2016), 219.

175 **"The Examen is a daily prayer":** Mark Thibodeaux, *Reimagining the Ignatian Examen: Fresh Ways to Pray for Your Day* (Chicago: Loyola, 2014).

178 **"You see, I believe":** Fred Rogers, "Fred Rogers Commencement Speech" (Marquette University, Milwaukee, WI, May 2001), https://tinyurl.com/29a8yjza.

179 **"God of herons and heartbreak":** Sarah Bessey, ed., "A Prayer to Learn to Love the World Again," in *A Rhythm of Prayer: A Collection of Meditations for Renewal* (New York: Convergent, 2021), 105.

Chapter 11: Repetition of Rest

185 **"The [biblical] writers":** Harper, *Very Good Gospel*, 31.
189 **"Jewish understanding of a day":** Warren, *Liturgy of the Ordinary*, 150–51.
193 **"rhythm of rest is not about legalism":** Abraham Joshua Heschel, *Sabbath: Its Meaning for Modern Man* (New York: Farrar, Straus and Giroux, 2005), 20.
195 **"at its heart, shame":** Harper, *Very Good Gospel*, 69.
196 **"Sufficiency isn't two steps up":** Lynne Twist, quoted in Brown, *Gifts of Imperfection*, 83.

Chapter 12: Counterpoint of Holidays

198 **"the process of coming back":** Joan Chittister, *The Liturgical Year: The Spiraling Adventure of the Spiritual Life* (Nashville: Thomas Nelson, 2009), 446.
199 **"Instead of a Hallmark calendar":** Sarah Bessey, *Out of Sorts: Making Peace with an Evolving Faith* (New York: Howard, 2015), 143.
199 **"Therefore, the question is not":** Warren, *Liturgy of the Ordinary*, 31.
200 **"The capital-*L* Liturgy":** James K. A. Smith, *You Are What You Love: The Spiritual Power of Habit* (Grand Rapids, MI: Brazos, 2016), 113.

200 **"goal of the church calendar":** Chittister, *Liturgical Year*, 276.

200 **"So if we need to be intentional":** Smith, *What You Love*, 113.

200 **"Examining my daily liturgy":** Warren, *Liturgy of the Ordinary*, 31.

202 **"Giving actually helps":** DeGroat, *Wholeheartedness*, 182.

205 **"Like the voices":** Chittister, *Liturgical Year*, 437.

206 **"Listen to your life":** Frederick Buechner, *Listening to Your Life: Daily Meditations with Frederick Buechner* (New York: HarperCollins, 1992), 2.

206 **"On Ash Wednesday":** Carolyn C. Brown, "Year B—Ash Wednesday (February 22, 2012)," *Worshiping with Children* (blog), January 16, 2012, https://tinyurl.com/466dc6kt.

208 **"I stretch out my hands":** Carol Reed-Jones, *Hildegard of Bingen: Woman of Vision* (Aston, PA: Paper Crane, 2004), 42.

210 **"keep our lives riveted":** Chittister, *Liturgical Year*, 450.